The PocketScroll® Series

SHAAR PRESS

IT
WAS'NT
HOW IT
SEEMED

Published by

Mesorah Publications, ltd

IT WASN'T HOW IT SEEMED

True stories about people who jumped to conclusions

by Yehudis Samet

Published by **SHAAR PRESS**
Distributed by MESORAH PUBLICATIONS, LTD.
4401 Second Avenue / Brooklyn, N.Y 11232 / (718) 921-9000
www.artscroll.com

ISBN 10: 1-57819-482-2 / ISBN 13: 978-1-57819-482-7

Printed in the United States of America by Noble Book Press

Dedicated to our Beloved Parents
Mr. and Mrs. Harry Walker

Whose creative vision and energetic leadership have launched and directed a multitude of worthy communal causes,

Whose commitment to Torah institutions and scholarship serve as an inspiration,

Whose boundless love and warmth envelop us and

Whose wisdom guides us.

We have no adequate words to thank you for the constant care and devotion you have showered upon us, your children, grandchildren, and great-grandchildren.

We are filled with admiration for all your achievements and your eagerness to assist others in every possible way.

May you be blessed with long, healthy, and happy years.

Table of Contents

Acknowledgments

My husband and I, together with our family, would like to express our appreciation:

To **Mrs. Blima Moskoff** for her efficient, creative, and pleasant assistance in typing and editing the original manuscript.

To **Yeshiva Ohr Samayach**, who ran a column entitled "The Other Side of the Story" in their "Ohrnet" publication. In response to "Ohrnet's" request for submissions, people around the world contributed their personal episodes, several of which have been included in these pages.

To the many individuals who wrote, faxed, and called, as well as those who approached me after a lecture or stopped me on a street corner, in a bank, at a wedding, or wherever, to enthusiastically share their own maddening encounters that turned out to have a terrific, never-imagined ending.

To our dear daughter **Tzirry**, for her invaluable contribution.

With humble and unbounded gratitude, we offer our thanks to the Almighty for enabling us to complete another book. May it be His will that the lessons herein increase understanding and respect amongst His children and bring honor to His Name.

Introduction

Why wouldn't he answer a simple question?
What nerve she has to ask for such a favor!
Would a normal person say something like that?
How could someone be so stingy...selfish...
extravagant...petty...irresponsible?

Some of us have a tendency to be highly critical and discontented, while others seem to have a more conciliatory nature, at peace with what life offers. However, from time to time we all encounter behavior that confounds or provokes us. In the Book of *Leviticus* (19:15), we are taught that when confronted with such a situation, "Judge your fellow man fairly." An additional admonition is given to us in *Ethics of the Fathers* (1:6), "Judge all people to the side of merit," that is, favorably.

What does judging others with favor mean? It means looking for a possible explanation, justification, or redeeming factor for behavior that appears unworthy or inappropriate. It means brainstorming for excuses that make sense and totally exonerate or leave us with at least a more positive feeling towards the offender.

The willingness to give others the benefit of the doubt is

an act of humility, an acknowledgement that the nature of human beings — and life itself — is too complex for us to erupt with haphazard, hasty verdicts. It is a recognition that while we may know a lot, we do not pretend to know everything.

Our trusty senses feed us information, but at times we can be fooled. I think I heard correctly. I know I saw what happened. And yet I might have misunderstood what was said or done. Might it be that I walked into the middle of a scene, confused and indignant, all because I missed a key word or event a moment before?

We often jump to erroneous conclusions because of one "small" detail unknown to us. One small but essential detail that completely changes the picture.

The skill of judging others with favor could really be called "The Art of Reconsidering." At time it means considering the possibility that the perpetrator intended no harm; he simply had not foreseen the consequences of his behavior. It occasionally means considering that this "villain" could be in pain or grappling with a problem that inhibits his ability to react as he normally would. Exercising our "good eye" prompts us to refocus and ponder, "Is *he* at fault, or is it our interpretation that is faulty?"

"Judge others to the side of merit" is a plea to seek out that merit, to look for the good in others despite their shortcomings. By concentrating on people's failings, we find ourselves surrounded by irritating, inconsiderate people. Our life is marred by consistent disappointments and aggravations. Zeroing in on people's strengths and positive qualities enables us to enjoy more people more and puts a spring back into our step.

When we make an effort to see people in a favorable light, we are confirming our understanding that although a particular behavior seems hurtful, lowly, or unreasonable, there may be another side to the story. True, there is evil in the world, and there are people who are incapable of rational behavior. Still we work with the premise that most of the people we deal with are, on the whole, decent and rational, *just as we feel we are.* We too can be guilty of gross insensitivity, selfishness, and a variety of reprehensible deeds; yet we usually claim "mitigating circumstances" or "guilty with an explanation." And just as we want others to reach out to us with understanding, to see us in a good light despite our faults and blunders (oh, how we need and even demand that consideration!), we owe the same to others.

Now, make no mistake. Giving the benefit of the doubt is not about defending evildoing. Nor does it mean whitewashing improper behavior. It certainly does not preclude taking action, defending our rights and the rights of others, or offering reproof. Rather, it means constantly reminding ourselves that things are not *always* the way they seem.

We were given this precept in order to help us build and

maintain a more peaceful society. Making the effort to climb into the other fellow's shoes, caring enough to argue his case, opens up vistas, enabling us to improve our relationships with co-workers, family members, neighbors, and friends. In truth, utilizing these tools brings harmony to every facet of our lives. Most significantly, when one's thoughts are peaceful, this is the beginning of true inner peace.

After the publication of *The Other Side of the Story*, we received letters and calls from people all over the world, telling us how the stories and strategies had changed their perspective. One person wrote about a broken friendship that had been mended as a result of her newfound skills. Another told how she "reconsidered" and knocked on the door of a neighbor whom she had previously shunned. Another related about how the principles that he had learned helped him forgive a close family member he had not spoken with in years. We heard episode after inspiring episode about people who gave others the benefit of the doubt and emerged as winners.

"We're waiting for more stories!" is what they told us.

So here they are.

The new stories you will read in the coming pages have been sent from various countries, from people young and old, from all walks of life and backgrounds. Although they are true, names and identifying details were changed to respect the privacy of persons involved.

There are few things that make a point stronger or more memorable than a story. We hope that reading these stories and their lessons will give you the skill to analyze troubling scenarios and then jump to (or at least arrive at) favorable conclusions. Insightful conclusions make it easier to deal with life's bumps and jabs in a more humble, peaceful way.

In the merit of our willingness to explain rather than complain, may those who have been hurt by *our* behavior be willing to consider different, kinder explanations for our offenses. May the Almighty help them see the best in us and judge us to the side of merit.

1.

Unwanted Guests

"**C**lose the door! Close the door!" my mother called out again and again from our bungalow's kitchen.

A breezeless summer afternoon in the country found our family and friends congregated in the sparsely furnished all-purpose room of our annual summer retreat.

My two married sisters were there with their husbands and children. My Uncle Bernie and Aunt Evelyn had driven up from the city. My brother, a lifeguard at a nearby camp, had the day off and had gotten a lift to our place. Some friends of my parents had surprised us and dropped in as well. Each received a whooping welcome and then pulled up a chair and joined us around the table.

My mother, not one to let herself be caught off guard, had made sure to fill her pots with plenty of extra food in anticipation of all the company.

While there was barely room around the table, there was also hardly an inch on the table. It would be easier to list what she might have inadvertently deleted than to attempt to describe the array of sumptuous dishes Mom managed to create in our tiny kitchen.

It was the kind of afternoon you savor and then reminisce about at the next occasion. Aside from the minor problems of the day, like running out of mustard, there was no fly in the ointment, except for the flies buzzing around the food, that is. They were spoiling Mom's tastefully laid luncheon, and no amount of shooing deterred them. Every time someone went in or out, it seemed a few more zoomed in to take their turn at the pickings.

Sympathizing with my mother's plight, some of us took up her chant, "Close the door, close the door," as yet another visitor walked in or out. I don't remember exactly when, but at some point my mother started calling the flies "unwanted guests." That struck all of us as funny — especially the children — and brought even more laughter to an already delightful afternoon. That is, until the following unfortunate incident occurred.

My mother was in the kitchen scooping out ice cream when Mr. Milner, our next door neighbor, came by to borrow something. Surrounded by children all anxious to get the biggest portion with the most sprinkles, Mom heard the squeak of the front door for the umpteenth time.

Holding up the dripping scoop, she shouted in our direction: "Fast! Close the door before any more unwanted guests come in!"

Standing there near the closed door, Mr. Milner's jaw dropped. Having been well used to the refrain, it took those assembled a second to realize what our neighbor thought he had heard. But before anyone was able to explain, Mr. Milner, thoroughly offended by this outrageous greeting, stomped out.

Of course, my father jumped up and ran right after him. After a long time my father came back. He said that Mr. Milner understood.

But you know, Mr. Milner never gave the children candies after that.

❧

We are all victims of the complexities of communication — the gap between what is being said and what is being heard. Like Mr. Milner, we have, upon occasion, been hurt and indignant all because of a miscommunication. In each case, giving the benefit of the doubt undoubtably would have been a great benefit.

2.

We Were Gypped

I wasn't taking any chances this time. I had it circled in red on my calendar and decided I would make this one memorable, especially since last year I forgot. Financially we were doing much better now, so I figured, all around, Ruthie deserved something special for our anniversary.

I know Ruthie likes me to surprise her. The problem arises when she doesn't like the surprise. To be more exact, she likes the surprise part, but not always my taste and originality. So I figured this time I had better do it right.

With only a few days left, I popped the question one morning before leaving for the office.

"How'd ya like a beautiful piece of gold jewelry?"

Let me tell you, one very happy wife followed me out to the car and kept waving as I turned out of the driveway.

I had already made some calls to find out where we could get a good deal. The name Sonya Arons was mentioned by a few friends. All the details checked out. She was nearby, had good prices, and top quality, so I called up for an appointment for that evening.

After dinner, Ruthie and I drove over. We ourselves were not sure what we wanted. Should we go for a necklace? A bracelet? Earrings? A pin? After about half an hour of selecting and rejecting, one of the bracelets caught Ruthie's eye, something new Sonya had just gotten in. Ruthie kept coming back to that piece and in the end we decided to take it.

Talk about happy! That was Ruthie. Talk about insurance payments — that was me. Kidding aside, although I spent more than I had originally planned, Ruthie's ear-to-ear grin made it all worthwhile.

Two weeks later, as I walked through the door, Ruthie greeted me. I could tell right away something was wrong. She reached into her pocket, pulled out the new bracelet, and dangled it in front of me. It wasn't hard to figure out the problem. One quick look told me the bracelet had corroded. The gold was peeling off.

Ruthie explained that after she had worn it, she put it in her drawer. A few hours ago she had taken it out and noticed that it was ruined. There was nothing more to say. Despite all the recommendations, we had been had.

That evening we drove back to Sonya's home, without an appointment. She opened the door, all smiles — until she saw our faces. I'm surprised she let us in, but she did, and even asked us to sit down. I ill-humoredly placed the bracelet on the table without a word. The sight of the flaky gold piece spoke much better than anything we could say.

Sonya walked over to the table and picked up the blighted bracelet. How would she worm her way out of this, I was thinking. What would she say to defend herself?

We watched her examine it over and under, shifting it back and forth.

Then, Sonya looked up and announced solemnly, "Mercury."

I wasn't sure I had heard her correctly.

"Mercury?" I repeated.

"Most probably. This bracelet must have been near mercury. That's the way gold looks when it comes in contact with that metal. Go home and check."

We did. When my wife opened her drawer, she found a broken thermometer and the pieces of mercury, just where the bracelet had been placed.

The universe is teeming with facts and phenomena unknown to most of us. How many people are aware, for example, of the effect of mercury on gold?

Being willing to consider that there may be some facts we are missing, that there may be another side to the story, makes our attempts at safeguarding our responses more pleasant for everyone.

In this way, judging favorably does not preclude taking action — it precedes it.

3.

Wrong Number

Just imagining the hooting and the rotten-tomato glances that would be thrown my way made me wince. Tomorrow will be the first of the month, and if I didn't walk in with those salary checks — oh, perish the thought. I didn't want to even think about it.

The bookkeeping of our well-staffed insurance firm was my responsibility. The last day of the month left behind a backlog of receipts, checks, bills, and tax forms, which gave me no choice but to drag home the books and finish the payroll at home. Facing my boss would be one thing, but the staff would be fit to be tied if I showed up empty-handed.

I dumped the ledgers on my desk, grabbed something from the fridge, and went right to work.

I was in the middle of calculating the hourly salaries when the phone rang. I would have ignored it, preferring not to break my concentration, but I was expecting a call from a friend about vacation plans, so I picked up.

A little girl was asking for the Goldstein family. "Sorry," I said, "you've got the wrong number."

I went back to my figures. The phone rang again. Same wrong number. I hung up, but a few minutes later the phone rang again. I already had a feeling who it was. Each time I picked up it was the voice of a little girl. She was making one call after another and asking for the Goldstein family. Maybe I should have said something, but that would have taken time that I didn't have.

How could I concentrate on numbers with all these interruptions? I started to lose my temper. Annoyed that I might miss my friend's call, but left with no choice, I took the phone off the hook and left it off for about an hour, certain that this would discourage her. But as soon as I put the phone back on the hook, she called again! I was ready to cry.

After about the seventh or eighth call, I threatened her that if she called one more time I would call the police.

At 6:30 p.m. the phone rang for about the tenth time. I picked it up, but remained silent. Again I could hear the voice of a little girl. What kind of parents would allow their child to do this all afternoon! I demanded to speak to her mother. To my surprise, she called her mother to the phone. Not hiding my feelings, I told the mother what her little girl had been doing to me all afternoon. The mother assured me that this was the first phone call her daughter had made that day. I'm sure she sensed from my sarcastic response that I did not buy her story. Despite my caustic comments, she was empathetic. Understanding my predicament, she wanted to be helpful. Maybe her daughter wasn't as innocent as she thought.

"Give me a few minutes to work this out," she offered good-naturedly. "I'll take your number and call you right back."

Sure enough, within five minutes she called and to my utter amazement this is what she said:

"My daughter's teacher gave all the girls in the class the phone number of their new teaching assistant, Esther Goldstein. The entire class of thirty girls was told to call the new assistant to find out if their trip would be taking place tomorrow as scheduled. The teacher apparently gave them the wrong number by mistake."

Until about 9:00 p.m. the phone still rang from time to time. Each time, it was a little girl wanting to know if the trip was on. Some girls, even after hearing that they had the wrong number, would still ask if there would be a trip. The payroll behind me, I answered everyone patiently and even cautioned them to remember their hats and bring plenty of water. Unable to withhold a little more advice, I told each one of those sweet, youthful voices that the most important thing was to hold onto their buddies and have a great time.

Our daily encounters can sometimes read like chapters in a mystery novel. In these cases, we already know who-

dunnit. Our job is primarily to discover why.

By making an effort to unravel the intricacies of human behavior, we provide ourselves with multiple benefits. Judging favorably helps us control our anger, uproot our grudges, and is the antidote to character assassination. Keeping us focused on solutions rather than recriminations enhances our physical and emotional health and promotes a life of peace.

4.

A Burned Reputation

Fifty years together is a landmark in anyone's book. After all is said and done, our dear parents are still pulling shoulder to shoulder. My father still ribs my mother that he got a real run for his money, and my mother, not one to take anything sitting down, kibbitzes that she got more that she bargained for.

We couldn't let this occasion pass without a celebration, so my three sisters and I decided to throw our parents an anniversary party. A few ideas were tossed around. Sima, the oldest, suggested using her huge backyard. We all agreed on the idea of renting a tent and having the party there.

It was my job to find the caterer. The first qualification was that it be someone who does small affairs. I remembered seeing such an ad in a community bulletin. I flipped through the classifieds, found the number, and dialed.

Mr. Y. answered. He was patient and courteous. He answered all my questions, and his price was right. However, I remembered Sima's parting words, "Get references." Mr. Y. gave me two references. I called, and both parties said they were very satisfied.

I proudly called Sima, confident that at least my job was taken care of successfully.

"Absolutely no way!" she declared adamantly. "I just heard that name. My neighbor was at an affair that he catered. I'm surprised he is still in business."

"Really?"

"Yes, really."

"This neighbor was at a bris he catered not long ago, and some of the food was burned."

"Burned?"

"That's right."

"You know, Sima, that's a serious accusation. You can ruin his business by spreading such a rumor."

"Maybe it's serious, but it's also true. There was a hall full of people there as witnesses. My neighbor and everyone else were served that burned food. Why don't you check it out yourself?"

"Sima, anyone can make a mistake. You can't disqualify him for one mistake."

"Listen," my sister continued, "no respectable, decent caterer serves burned food. There's no excuse for that. Even if he had to go out and buy more food at the last minute. And anyway, what if he does it at our party? Are you willing to take responsibility that he won't?"

Now it sounded different. How could I take that responsibility? If he had done it once, he could…do it again.

Can you think of a valid excuse for burning food? I really couldn't. I was ready to drop him.

It was my sister, always fair, who started having pangs of conscience about ruining someone's reputation. She called up her neighbor and got the name of the people who had made that bris. When they got on the line, she explained that she was calling about Mr. Y. who had catered their bris. To her amazement they immediately answered that they recommend him highly.

"But — but — I heard he burned some of the food," she stammered.

From the other end my sister heard a small gasp and then, "I'm so glad you called. What a terrible misunderstanding! Let me explain. Mr. Y. was already booked for the day we needed him and did not have a big enough staff to cater two affairs on the same day. I knew he was really good, and I didn't want to give up easily. So I asked him if he could prepare the food and we would reheat it ourselves. He explained patiently that he didn't work that way, but I begged and pleaded. I must have caught him in a weak moment or something, because finally — reluctantly — he gave in.

"I never dreamed people would blame the caterer," she said with obvious misgiving. "We were the ones who burned the food."

Playing around with someone's reputation is like playing with fire, though we may not give it a second thought. Giving people the benefit of the doubt means pausing to deliberate and reconsider and to really give it that second thought. If we are willing to leave it open — for the meantime — then we will be more inclined to check out a rumor for accuracy before we throw someone into the bonfire, burning his good name to a crisp.

5.

Getting the Fax Straight

We wanted an office that would be an easy commute, so after investigating several options, we took a home improvement loan from our local bank and hired a contractor to remodel our basement. You can't get much closer to home than that.

Thus began three long months that taxed all the senses. All day long, we had workers tracking up and down the stairs with their various requests and dirty shoes. Wafts of tar mixed with paint, dust blended with sawdust, and the shrill sound of the electric saw competed with the earsplitting music the construction crew couldn't seem to forego. The hours we spent without a water supply or with the electricity shut off gave us a new appreciation of the basic amenities we had previously taken for granted.

And then finally, one day, it was all over, and peace returned to our humble abode. The day the workers left, we brought in a desk, a computer, one swivel chair, two folding chairs, a postage machine, a filing cabinet, and two posters — one of the Swiss Alps and the other a panoramic view of the Grand Canyon. With that we launched our home-based travel agency.

Oh, the adventure of travel. The allure of the unknown, the charm of the unfamiliar, the appeal of the beyond. Maybe you conjure up the same images I had — first class cabins, five-star hotels, all-expense-paid vacations — all at my fingertips.

No one prepared us for the downside.

"Hello, Mr. Heller. This is Joe Brown. I'm calling from Amsterdam. No, I didn't realize it's three in the morning. I'm here in Schiphol Airport. My connecting flight was canceled. What should I do?"

Or how about this one that my wife got?

"Hi, Mrs. Heller. This is Sally Green. My flight is leaving in a few hours, and I'm overweight. Can you help me?"

Don't say it. Never say the first thing that comes to your mind. Not to Sally, and not to friends who want their tickets at cost, neighbors who request an extra suitcase for every member of their party, or close relatives who tell you that they would like to use your services, but they have a policy not to do business with family. Our responses require discretion, foresight, hindsight, insight, and a genuine willingness to understand the other position.

We had a customer — one of our long-standing VIPs — who booked two rooms in a most luxurious hotel at $1400 a day for two and a half weeks. Only with pull could I get her in altogether, since it was the height of the season. But for such a customer, you use any pull you can. I explained to her that it was a prepaid, no-refund booking. I made it very clear that our agency was guaranteeing and that once I confirmed there was no reneging. Three days into the vacation, she called me to say she doesn't like the service at the hotel. She's packing and checking out. Just like that. Stunned (make a quick calculation of $1400 times eighteen days!), I reminded her about the no-refund clause. What do you think she answered? She claimed I should have known she wouldn't like it there!

All right, I'm the first one to admit it was my own fault. In business, sometimes you learn the hard way. Today, even our best customers pay in advance. I'd rather lose the account but keep my shirt. (By the way, in case you're curious, that disgruntled client did pay up — mostly.)

Just last month our fax machine rebelled. Always prone to stubborn fits of dysfunction, our old fax/phone finally put in for retirement.

All too familiar with the importance of dealing with reputable people, I was looking to purchase a new machine from an established and reliable company. I called around. The name that kept coming up was HomeTec. Several different sources reported that HomeTec had a well-established, well-earned reputation for quality machines and prompt service. We decided to go with them.

I called the office and made an appointment with a sales-person for the following morning.

After hearing the description of the machine we needed, he showed me the fax/phone models available. I liked what I saw and I picked one out. He gave me a demonstration. It seemed easy enough.

"Just follow the instructions," he smiled affably as he handed me the manual. I put my new purchase in the trunk of my car and drove home.

I'm not especially mechanical, but since we had owned a fax machine before, I assumed there would be no problem. Boy, was I wrong.

I set up the machine just the way the salesman explained. It didn't work. I fiddled, reread, and re-reread the booklet. No go.

I called HomeTec. They advised me to bring it in. So I shlepped it back. They plugged it in, and it worked. You know how you feel when that happens. They were very nice, but I slunk out with a feeling of gross inadequacy.

Back in the office, I plugged in the machine. It did not work. I called back and insisted that a repairman come.

After checking it out, the HomeTec technician admitted that — for some reason even he could not figure out — it really did not work in my house. He was very accommodating, just like their reputation had promised. He called the office, and they told me to come down and get a new machine. Which I did.

Once again, I lugged a machine down the stairs, lifted it out from between the protective layers of styrofoam, placed it on the desk, plugged it in, and tried it out. Three problems were immediately apparent. First of all, the seven-button stuck when pressed. That meant we could not dial any number with a seven in it. Second, the button under the receiver stuck. Whenever I tried to answer the phone or make a call, the button did not release, which meant the phone continued to ring until I pulled up the button manually. I will admit, not a major problem, but we had paid a hefty price for a new machine. Everything was supposed to work.

Most disturbing was the cord. If I moved the phone cord in the wrong way, my calls were cut off.

This was getting ridiculous.

"Listen..." I began when the HomeTec salesman answered my call.

Although he patiently heard me out, as I enumerated the defects in our new fax, he was not sure what to do. He transferred me to the manager.

"I know you have a good reputation. What's going on?" I asked him.

Of course, he was very apologetic and promised me that he would send over his best technician.

Tool box in hand, the man arrived early the next day and spent a long time checking every part of the problematic machine. After more than an hour, he closed the cover and showed me that everything was all taken care of. I stood there and watched his demonstration closely. Packing up his tools and assuring me all would be well, he left. He was a nice guy. I wanted to believe him.

The rest of the day, all indeed went well. My hopes soared high that the problem was finally solved.

The next day I was in the middle of a conversation with Michael Fields. We were negotiating the details of a tour he wanted me to put together for a group of his associates.

Then in mid-sentence, we were cut off.

I flew off the handle. This one cuts people off too! Isn't there a limit? Mine had been reached.

When I finally got the HomeTec manager on the line, I bellowed into the phone, "I don't know how you got your reputation! Do you know what kind of loss I'm incurring because of your incompetence? How can I do business with people if I can't have a straight conversation! I'm not interested in any more repairs. I expect you to deliver a new machine — one that works!"

Not even waiting for a response, I hung up.

Two minutes later, the phone rang.

"Heller? This is Michael Fields."

I knew it would be Fields, and I knew what he was going to say. I only hoped he was not too upset about being cut off.

"I'm really sorry about what happened," Fields excused himself. "I was on a cell phone, and my battery went dead."

How could Mr. Heller have known otherwise? How could he have been expected to refrain from drawing the wrong conclusion? Granted, it seems almost unavoidable. However, the outburst wasn't.

Before we scream "foul play," we should think about the embarrassment we cause ourselves in case, just in case, we are wrong. With that in mind, most probably we will at least scream more softly.

6.

A Bone to Pick

An acquaintance of mine made a stinging remark that was so terribly hurtful that even today, months later, the pain has not completely subsided.

We were sitting together at a charity fund-raising tea when it happened. The room was exquisitely arranged. Each table was covered with a cloth of delicate lace and adorned with a centerpiece of tea roses in a pewter vase. Antique china teacups graced each setting, alongside individual ceramic teapots topped with charming quilted covers. A three-tier silver tray offering triangular cucumber tea sandwiches, dainty cookies and sweets, and tiny pieces of exotic fruit symmetrically placed, attested to the handiwork of a devoted committee who had spared no effort nor overlooked a single detail that would enhance the success and beauty of the affair.

So there we were, ten of us sitting around a table. We were all old friends, many of us bumping into each other weekly; others only at functions like this one. The conversation was animated, the mood festive. This was one of those times when, for a few hours, you could forget your appointments, carpooling, housework, homework, and job. You could just relax and enjoy the elegant ambience and easy camaraderie.

Then without any warning, she said it. Right there, in front of us all.

Everyone looked at me to see how I would react. I'm sure I turned red. But I would not give her the satisfaction of knowing how much the comment hurt. I pulled myself together and somehow got through another half-hour.

Then I could not bear the humiliation a moment longer. I picked myself up — I can't even remember if I said goodbye to anyone — and drove home.

For days, that insult replayed itself in my mind, dancing in front of me mockingly. I wouldn't call her, and I would not forgive her either. If she wanted to apologize, she knew my number. But the call never came.

So the hurt was just there, weighing down inside of me. Every once in a while, it got caught in my throat. I wanted to push it down or get it out, but I did not know how.

Then something else happened recently. This time I was not the victim, but the perpetrator. Besides remorse, it also left me with something to think about.

Ella Stark and I met at a wedding, where we were seated next to each other. Between eating and dancing, we chatted and discovered that we were neighbors of sorts, the Starks living in an adjoining community. My husband had to get home, so I said goodbye to Ella, explaining that we were leaving early. She perked up when she heard these words and quickly told me that the people who had driven her to the wedding were staying later, and she was looking for a ride home. Perhaps we had room, since she was also anxious to get home. I checked with my husband to make sure he had not promised the place to someone else. It was okay, and the three of us made our way to the parking lot. As we approached the car, I realized there was going to be a problem.

Our car is a two-door sub-compact. Ella Stark is a tall, heavy woman. How would she maneuver herself into the back seat? I wondered. I was not sure if I should suggest that she sit in the front. Maybe that would embarrass her and it would surely be awkward. So I let it go.

With considerable difficulty, Ella laboriously pushed herself through the narrow passage and planted herself on the back seat. Much relieved, I repositioned my seat and got in.

As we were riding, the conversation turned in many directions. We spoke about mutual friends, community events, the shortest route home, the telephone strike, and of course, about the joyous wedding we had just attended.

It was then that Ella mentioned her daughter's wedding that was to take place in three days. She explained that the reason she was rushing home was because she still had so much to take care of. They had a last gown fitting scheduled for the next morning. Ella still had not found shoes to match her dress. They had not finished tallying response cards, and there was still the seating to arrange. By the time she had finished her extensive list of to-do's, I was a bit dizzy wondering how she would get to all that in just three days. I was amazed at how this woman could get out to another wedding while so much was going on in her life. Me? Three days before a daughter's wedding? If I had been in her place, I would not go anywhere at all.

By that time we had pulled up in front of her home. While she was thanking us and gathering her things, I was still marveling at her ambitiousness. It was then that I turned around and said in wonderment, "I just can't imagine how you can manage to get out."

At first I could not understand why her face clouded over. She sat there not saying a word.

Confused, I got out of the car and pulled my seat forward. Once again, Ella struggled to get up and renegotiate the narrow passageway, and then without another word, she walked away.

I turned towards my husband who explained what I had done.

Clearly, Ella was hurt and deserved an apology. Yet I felt I could not call. Bringing it up again would only make it worse. What could I possibly say to appease her?

I see myself as a nice, kind, normal human being, and yet I just said something that came out sounding nasty. Maybe I did not mean it the way it sounded, but the victim, that poor woman, does not know that. I feel incapable of making amends. Nonetheless, I would like to be forgiven, reinstated as an "upstanding member of the human race."

It was this incident and the predicament in which it left me that enabled me to rethink that deep humiliation I had suffered at the tea. "If she wanted to apologize, she could always phone," I remembered thinking with anger. And yet I never did make that call. Could she also have had a similar excuse or maybe something else to say for herself?

Someone once told me that judging others with favor is like the Heimlich maneuver. It helps dislodge resentments that are stuck inside and just will not go away. Very often we do not have the skill, the know-how, to dislodge that "bone" of contention — until we find ourselves in similar circumstances of guilt. By remembering the excuses we had for ourselves, and having the willingness to share these excuses with the wrongdoer, we can often effectively dislodge our anger and relieve our distress.

7.

Smile for the Camera

"If we are already investing, it's worthwhile spending a few more bucks to get something solid," my husband Saul sagaciously concluded. After soliciting advice from his friends, checking out consumers' magazines, and pounding a lot of pavement, Saul finally made his choice.

And now our new camera was missing.

The last time we remembered seeing it was one of those Sundays, when we took it to our family get-together. We have a standing invitation to the home of our youngest daughter Miriam, who invites all of us over on Sunday afternoons. It's a barbecue in the summer, pizza and homemade soup in the winter. Then Saul and I spend time with our grandchildren, sometimes treating them to a trip to the zoo or a park. The camera always accompanies us on these frequent visits and outings, and on all excursions. Recently, we put together several albums, and any and all visitors to our house are presented with a visual history of all our wonderful memories. You can well imagine how much our camera means to us.

Where could it be? We both remembered taking it home that day. I checked the car. I pulled everything out of the closet where it was usually kept. We searched in a few other less likely places. Nothing.

Could we both remember bringing it home and still be wrong? I called Miriam. Her family promised to conduct a thorough search.

The next day Miriam called back. They had sent the children on a scouting mission, even offering them an attractive reward, but the camera did not turn up.

I combed our house. No luck. Weeks went by. Saul took out our old camera that does not take good pictures. It would have to suffice. Every time we wanted to photograph something, we were reminded of our loss.

Truthfully, I do not like to suspect anyone without proof, but after checking every other possibility, I could not push away my suspicions that Florie, our cleaning help, had a hand in this.

No, we had never actually caught her taking anything, but the year before, my sister was visiting and had left an expensive necklace on the dresser. Florie was cleaning that day and had straightened up the room. We never saw that necklace again. Besides that, I cannot find a pair of good pearl earrings, and a piece of silver is missing from the breakfront.

I know you will tell me that I had no proof, and I agree. But I will explain why I felt there was a good possibility that

Florie had pilfered the camera. Florie always compliments us on our possessions. I know she has very little money and considers us "the haves" while she counts herself amongst the "have nots." In addition, she knew that we have two cameras, while she had none. This way, if she takes ours, we both have one! In trying to judge her favorably, I reason that maybe she sees this as fair.

Once this suspicion took root in me, I was, of course, uncomfortable. It was very unpleasant having Florie work for me every week with this glaring doubt concerning her honesty hanging over me. You may wonder why I did not let her go. The fact is that Florie is an easygoing woman, a good cleaner, and a self-starter. I never have to give her directions. She always knows just what to do. So I was reluctant to send her packing.

I decided that one way to tackle the problem was to let her know that I suspected her. Once she knew that I knew, then maybe she would consider slipping the camera back into our house, and the matter would be put to rest. So one day, while she was eating lunch and I was putting away groceries, I very nonchalantly mentioned our missing camera and added that if she ever happened to come across it, she should let me know. From the uneasy look on Florie's face, I could tell that she got the point. The question was whether or not her conscience would bother her enough to make her do something about rectifying her mistake. I got the answer. Although she still came every week, the camera never showed up.

Not long after that, we flew to the West Coast to visit our son for three weeks. Before we left, Miriam asked us if we could leave our car with her for the time we would be away. Of course we were happy to do her the favor.

The day before our return, Miriam brought the Ford to our car wash, so they could get it back in shape for our return. No doubt a variety of snacks and treats had been enjoyed in our back seat during three weeks of chauffeuring her children — and most likely some other people's children also.

We arrived home to find our refrigerator stocked with immediate necessities. Our ever-thoughtful daughter also included a mushroom quiche, one of my favorites, and the oatmeal bars that Saul enjoys. The car stood in the driveway looking none the worse for the wear or additional mileage.

The next day, Saul and I went out to the supermarket to stock up our empty pantry. After filling up the trunk to its capacity, we went to put the remaining packages on the back seat. When we opened the door, a surprise awaited us. There on the seat sat our camera.

Immediately, we called Miriam.

"We are just thrilled, honey," I cried with delight into the phone. "So you finally found it. Tell me, where was it?"

"Where was what, Mom?" Miriam asked uncertainly.

"The camera, of course" I laughed.

"Camera? What camera?" My daughter repeated herself, sounding more confused.

"Miriam, dear, the camera we have been missing. It was on the back seat of the car. Didn't you put it there?"

"Back seat? I didn't know anything was in the back seat. I took the car straight from your car wash and parked it in the driveway. I never even looked into the back seat."

This was the second big surprise for me in the last five minutes.

"Why don't you call the car wash, Mom? What's the guy's name? Ken? Maybe he knows how it got there."

I went straight for the phone.

"Hello, can I please speak to Ken?" I waited.

"Hello, Ken? This is Mrs. Lerner. I'm fine, thank you, and you? Ken, my daughter brought in our car for washing, and there was a camera on the seat. Did you hap-"

"Yessirree, Mrs. Lerner," Ken interrupted. "That car was sure dirty. I did a real thorough job for you. As I was cleaning under the front seat I saw this case. There was a camera inside. I just left it on the seat in the back. Hope that was OK, Mrs. Lerner."

When Florie came that week, I told her that we had found the camera. I thought she would be pleased, but instead she flashed me a hard look and turned away.

Later that week an electrician came to do some work

upstairs in the bedrooms. We were having trouble with fuses that kept blowing. He checked all the rooms. When he got to the guest room, he moved the dresser in order to test the outlet on that wall. There on the floor was my sister's necklace.

❧

How often is household help blamed for taking things we ourselves misplaced?

Before you throw out an accusation, even a subtle one, be careful. Consider the number of times in your own life you suspected people of taking things and subsequently discovered the "stolen" item in the glove compartment, forgotten at the dentist, at the bottom of the bag you rarely use, lent to a neighbor, or in your own top drawer.

8.

Rage on the Road

I am sure that you are all too familiar with the well-published and much-discussed phenomenon called "road rage," a reference to drivers who become impatient, irritated, frustrated, enraged; their emotions escalate out of control, endangering themselves and others on the road.

Well, I am road rage personified. Or rather, I used to be. Let me tell you when I started to change my attitude.

My wife and I were riding in the car one Sunday morning. Halfway to our destination we came to an area where there was heavy construction, one of those places where they have been building as long as you can remember.

As a result, there was one narrow lane running the length of the site with, of course, no possibility to pass. We were late and the car in front of us was barely creeping.

I tightened my grip on the wheel.

"Some people don't belong on the road," I snarled as I hit the horn.

My wife tried to calm me down but I was not in the mood to listen. She is into this "judging favorably" thing but I'm not up to it when it comes to people behind the wheel who don't know how to drive.

"There are so many reasons why people can't go fast," she began brightly. I just glared at her.

"Maybe someone in the car is holding a pot of chicken soup," she suggested imaginatively. I kept my eyes straight ahead but I was picturing her satisfied smile, as she sat there reveling in her creative solution.

"No, really," she continued, knowing full well against whom she was pitted. "My friend told me this great story. Once she was annoyed at a slow driver. When she finally pulled up alongside her at a red light, my friend rolled down her window and yelled something nasty. The driver quickly bent over and then held up a small tank filled to the top with fish and water."

My wife's attempts at appeasing me were not having their desired effect. I just honked louder and longer.

"Even with a pot of chicken soup they wouldn't go this slow," I growled, craning my neck to see where the construction ended.

A half mile later a second lane opened, and the snail-like procession was over. As I pulled ahead, you can be sure I slowed down enough to give my leisure-paced lead one last long horn blast, together with an insufferable leer.

The driver heard me all right and saw me too, but it was not like he was even offended. He just pointed to something

I could not identify and continued at that nerve-racking pace. As he was motioning, I suddenly became aware of a dull thud-like noise — a thump ... thump ... thump ... thump. My wife heard it too. My eyes followed the direction of his finger, and I spotted the source of that irritating sound. He was pointing at his flat tire.

As we drove along I snuck a look at my helpmate. So far she had not said anything. I was hoping she would let me off graciously. A few more miles of silence and I could not take it anymore. "Okay, okay," I gave in. "You can add this to your theories. Put it right after soup and fish tanks."

I'll tell you one thing. Maybe I still get a little annoyed behind the wheel, but never when my wife is sitting next to me.

❧

How can we hope to give the benefit of the doubt, if to us there is no doubt?

"Doubt" is defined as a deliberate suspension of judgment. The first step, then, is to allow for that doubt by permitting ourselves a minute for a second thought.

We can turn a wrong-doing into a "doubt" by acknowledging that there may be a mitigating factor unknown to us: Maybe he did it but feels sorry; maybe he did not know it was wrong, or at least how wrong; maybe he wanted to explain, but had no time, or was too embarrassed; maybe we were to blame, or at least partially to blame; maybe if we were in his place, we wouldn't do much better.

Our goal is to give the benefit of the doubt. We have defined "doubt." How do we define "benefit?" "Benefit" is the kindness we extend to others by our willingness to leave room for doubt.

9.

Taken for a Ride

The note was folded in half. He pressed it into my hand as he greeted me with a cheerier "Hello," than usual. I knew the paper had to be announcing a class trip or some school party or celebration. What else would produce such a beaming smile and shining eyes?

I wasn't wrong. The note informed us of an upcoming trip to a farm, culminating a three-month social studies unit about life on a farm.

It had been fun helping him collect and analyze labels on packages of cheese, and relearning what I had forgotten about pasteurization. Even more thrilling was learning together with Avi so many facts I had never been taught. Did you know that if you take a raw egg and hold it in the center of your palm, it will not crack, no matter how hard you squeeze? (Just make sure to do it over the sink.)

Accepting the pen Avi was so anxiously holding out to me, I signed the permission slip with pleasure. "Put it right in your briefcase, so you won't lose it or forget it," I warned my son, handing it back to him.

That night as he lay in bed too excited to sleep, we talked about silos, hay, troughs, and tractors, and how chickens hatch eggs. We talked and talked until I saw his eyelids drooping and finally shut.

The next morning I packed up Avi's lunch and some extras for the longer hours he would be gone. Planting a kiss on his forehead, I watched as he raced down the block to the school bus.

When he was no longer visible, I grabbed my coat and hurried off to work.

From the minute I stepped into the office, the phone did not stop ringing. I could barely catch my breath between calls. We had advertised for a new executive secretary. Judging from the number of responses coming in, it must have sounded like quite an attractive position.

As it was, not one of the applicants seemed particularly promising. This last call, however, took the cake. Why call if you have no skills, no qualifications, no training, and no recommendations?

At times like these my mother would surely have reminded me, "Estie, if you put yourself in the other person's shoes, your trek through life will be more pleasant." Taking her advice, I tried to imagine what this unqualified caller had in mind when she applied. Maybe she figured her great personality would win us over, and we would be willing to train her on the job.

Before I got any further in my conjectures, the phone rang again and that was the end of my theorizing for the time being.

I probably would have skipped lunch, but I had to mail some urgent letters. So I decided to take a trip over to the post office, and maybe grab some cake and coffee on the way.

Coming out of the building, I headed for my car parked across the street. As I stood by the curb, fishing in my bag for the keys, a school bus came rumbling down the street. I might not have noticed it had it not been for the noise. What rowdy children!

I opened the car door and slid behind the wheel. Would you believe it, even with the closed windows I could hear those children yelling.

As I turned the key and looked into the mirror, I could see the bus almost alongside me. I tell you, those children had their mouths right up to the opening of the windows and were screaming their lungs out. Where were their teachers? Who was watching them?

Curious to know where these kids were from, I looked for the name of the school on the bus. There, across the side of the bus, was printed "North County Academy."

When we had moved into the community three years before, one of the first things we did was investigate our educational options. We had made many inquiries until we had it narrowed down to two possibilities. Although one school was located a longer bus ride away, its many advantages outweighed that drawback.

We found out that some of the finest families in the community sent their children there. The scholastic level was high, and the building was large and well kept. Most important to us, the administration was caring and professional, and the educational staff was known to be outstanding.

Having just witnessed the behavior of the children from the school we had rejected, and the teachers' apparent tolerance of it, this incident convinced me further that we had made the right choice.

Back at the office I concluded that the danish and cappuccino were also the right choice, because they energized me and gave me the patience to deal with several long-winded applicants.

When I arrived home later, I found a message on the answering machine, saying that the trip was running behind schedule, and the children would be home later than originally expected. That considerate call saved me some unnecessary worrying.

Two hours later than expected, Avi ran up the steps, dropped his things in the hall, and let out a resounding, "MOMMY!" Hearing the clinking of the dishes and the running water, he made a beeline for the kitchen. He started telling me all about his trip, talking excitedly and breathlessly. I tried to interrupt long enough to offer him something to eat, but he would have none of that. He wanted to tell all, then and there.

Pulling me to the table, he insisted on my undivided attention. He told me about the cows, milking machines, udders, barns, stalls, pastures, scarecrows hay, and what have you. By all appearances, he had had a whale of a time.

Then he proceeded to describe the chicken coop.

"Mommy," he said, his eyes open wide in amazement. "The farmer explained to us that chickens lay eggs, about one a day or so, until they have twenty to thirty eggs, and that's called a clutch, and then she sits on them, all thirty at once!" After that one long, run-on sentence, Avi stopped for a second to see if I was duly impressed. Apparently satisfied with my reaction, he sped on.

"She mixes the clutch all the time. She moves the middle eggs to the outside and nudges the outside ones to the middle, and she knows which one is which! It's like a rotation system, and every egg gets turned a few times a day."

He needed to stop again, for some air, and then continued on and on about the chickens. Despite my prodding, he didn't seem to want to move on to another subject, although I was sure he had seen other things that day.

After awhile my suspicions were awakened. I sensed from his mischievous smile that he was hiding something. What was up his sleeve?

There's nothing like a mother's intuition, that's all I can say. After a few minutes, he couldn't hold it in anymore.

"Mommy, I have two surprises for you," he finally blurted out. Without further ado, Avi headed for the hall and came back with a box. "Each kid gets a chance to bring one home for two days," he said as he opened the lid and lifted out a tiny chick for his startled mother to see. To run no risk, it came along with food and instructions for care. My son was thrilled beyond belief.

"Oh, how exciting," I smiled broadly, trying to match his enthusiasm. "And what is the second surprise, Avi?" I asked, wondering what could possibly top the first one. He certainly had piqued my curiosity.

Cautiously, Avi put down the box.

"You know why we were late?"

I shook my head, honestly clueless.

"There was a mix-up, and the bus that was supposed to take us broke down. Everyone was disappointed, but after a while they got a bus, and we started out late. The best part," — he smiled broadly and paused, giving me that fraction of a second to imagine what could be "best" for him — "was that on the way, we passed your office!"

Passing my office was not something he did every day, so I took for granted that that was the surprise he was referring to.

"That's nice, honey."

"No, that's not all," he continued. "When we turned down your street, I told my friends that you work on that block, and then you know what?"

"What?" I echoed, genuinely enjoying his tale. Apparently, there was more "surprise" in store.

"Exactly that minute you came out of the building. I saw you first, then one of my friends called, 'Avi, isn't that your Mom?' The whole bus heard and everyone looked and then decided to say hello. We hollered and screamed, until our teacher finally managed to quiet us down. But by that time you were busy starting up the car and didn't notice us."

There was no way that Avi could have picked up my train of thought when I asked him questions about the bus.

"Yeah, that's right. How did you know that the bus was from North Country Academy? When we broke down our principal called up theirs, and asked if we could borrow their extra bus, so we wouldn't have to miss the trip."

At times like this my mother would surely say, "Estie, when you put two and two together, make sure you don't come out to five."

In this story, Estie added on one more reason, extra proof to validate her choice of schools. But her addition was wrong. The school she chose for her children may, in fact,

have been a better choice for her family, but this time, at least, her evidence was faulty.

Estie wonders how a person could apply for a job, without the required skills. Yet, she, together with many of us, is willing (even anxious) to undertake the position of judge, passing judgment with pitifully few skills.

10.

In the Un-Easy Chair

We were holding a big fund-raiser for an important community cause. As co-chairman of the evening, I headed a committee of dedicated men who performed far beyond the call of duty. I felt they all deserved public acknowledgment, and therefore I took special care to cite each one of them individually when writing up my opening remarks.

The big evening arrived. The committee worked until the last minute, reviewing every detail to ensure that everything would run smoothly.

Although we managed to start more or less on time, a problem developed with the sound system which took half an hour to fix, throwing us off schedule. To make matters worse, the first speaker spoke 15 minutes overtime.

I was next. As I gathered my notes, the president approached me, saying that the keynote speaker needed to catch a plane. Since we were behind schedule, I could speak for five minutes — and no more.

Unnerved and flustered, I hesitantly stepped up to the

podium. What could I delete at this last minute? Everything I had prepared was important. With no time to think, I simply began at the beginning. After five minutes I got a wave from the president to wind up. I fumbled with a closing thought, and sat down.

At the end of the evening, my co-chairman walked over to me.

"Joe, I'm surprised at you," he said in a voice full of reproach. "You of all people should know how important it was to thank those who helped. You, more than anyone, saw how they came through day and night, whenever they were needed, and always at a moment's notice. They turned this evening into a success and they deserved public recognition."

As much as I tried to interrupt, I couldn't get a word in edgewise. Finally, when he finished saying what he felt he had to say, he gave me a chance to speak, and I explained what had happened.

But what I really wanted to say was: "While we're on the topic of 'should have known,' you should have known me well enough to know that I do understand the importance of appreciation. Of course I know that these people should have been thanked. Why couldn't *you* judge me favorably? Couldn't you give me the benefit of the doubt?"

❧

The best way to be convinced of the importance of judging favorably is to be the one suspected. Being in a position where onlookers assume we are doing one thing, while we know something quite different is going on, teaches us how easy it is to reach the wrong conclusions.

11.

A Friend in Need, Indeed

My first-grade daughter was home with the chicken pox. Our doctor had prescribed an antihistamine to relieve the itching. The tablets were pale pink with colorful speckles.

That afternoon, a friend came by to visit me, and we were sitting together in the living room engrossed in conversation. After a while, I realized that my two-year-old son, Daniel, was much too quiet... a sure sign of trouble. A bit of searching brought me to the kitchen, where I discovered Daniel sitting untroubled under the table, munching the last of his sister's attractive pink pills.

I panicked. When my first-grader saw me starting to lose it, she ran to me and began sobbing.

I knew I had to take control of myself. Running to the phone, I dialed "911." They connected me to "Poison Control." While I was still on the phone, I noticed my friend making a hasty exit out the front door. I made a mental note of her desertion but was too distraught to think about it any further.

In the meantime I tried pounding Daniel on the back. That didn't work. I put my finger down his throat. Out came lots of pink pills.

A police car and an ambulance arrived within minutes to rush us to the emergency room. Daniel was thrilled with his escorts and the sirens and seemed to be in great spirits. I was still worried about what the doctor might find in him. As we sped along, my mind wandered back to the scene of my "friend" running out, leaving me alone at such a difficult moment, showing her true colors when I needed her support.

When we arrived at the hospital, Daniel was given a thorough checkup. Everything seemed to be OK, and it was not too long before we were discharged.

About five minutes after we came home, the phone rang. It was my "friend." At first I felt like slamming down the phone, but to my credit, I had enough control to listen to her.

It's a good thing I didn't hang up or blow up. It took only a minute of listening to learn that the deserter was actually a friend indeed. After hearing my assurances that Daniel was fine, she described with great emotion how she had raced home and returned breathlessly with what she thought was the proper antidote, just as the ambulance was pulling away. And she was never the wiser that I had ever considered otherwise.

❧

Although some people are very judgmental and others less so, all of us have times when we question people's behavior. When such a situation presents itself, judging favorably is a tool to help us consider reasonable alternatives.

When we find ourselves:

❖ *Censuring — How could she refuse, when I've done so much for her?*

❖ *Discrediting — We all managed to come, why couldn't she?*

❖ *Disapproving — That's the way you treat parents... raise children ... entertain guests?*

... that's when giving the benefit of the doubt comes to play.

12.

Eating His Heart Out

Every Thursday evening my wife and I treat ourselves to an evening out. We both have frenetic schedules that keep us running in and out, often meeting only at the front door, with a quick hello and goodbye. Eve and I agree that by the end of the week, it's time to touch base, and if we don't consider our weekly date as etched in stone, it just won't happen.

So we do just that, giving ourselves time to catch our breath, unwind, and tune in to what's happening in each other's life.

Although occasionally opting for Chinese or Italian cuisine, mostly we are steady customers at a small steakhouse where the service is good, the food tasty, and the ambience quiet and relaxing.

In the back of the room off to the left, there is an open grill, where a chef is stationed, grilling to order. Strategically positioned, its wafts are meant to stimulate the olfactory centers and whet the appetite.

The maitre d' pointed to a table for two on the far side of the room, where we could have a little more privacy.

Satisfied with his suggestion, we followed his lead as he ushered us across the floor.

As we made our way, we passed a couple, also at a table for two, chatting quietly, his cane hooked to the back of the chair.

I might not have noticed them, or the cane, except that as I passed, I heard a clatter. Turning back, I saw that I had apparently brushed against the chair and knocked the cane to the floor. I quickly retraced my footsteps. Replacing the stick on the chair back, I exchanged smiles with two pairs of gentle eyes, which had scores of years to their credit. I acknowledged their thanks with an unpretentious nod and continued on to our table.

The waiter scurried off and returned promptly with a breadbasket and ice water. Smiling across the table to Eve, the driving force behind this weekly commitment, I reminded myself to thank her for encouraging us to do this.

The waiter presented himself once more, menus in hand. We each accepted the somewhat superfluous offer. By this stage of the game, we probably could rattle off the selections by heart. We scanned the pages perfunctorily and then went on to order our usuals.

As I handed back my menu, I glanced over to that couple we had passed and noticed that they hadn't been waited on. There was nothing on the table — no menu, no bread, and no water in the glasses.

Strange. They had come in before us. Quite certainly not

the pushy types, they probably would not speak up for themselves but would rather sit patiently, waiting to be noticed.

But why should they have to beg for service? They were certainly as deserving as anyone else.

OK. Enough. Tonight is for Eve. Do not let yourself be distracted, I reminded myself. You came to relax. There is enough tension and problem-solving in the office all day. This is time out. Keep it that way.

I took a deep breath and pulled my mind back to our own table. The waiter brought our orders. I snuck a look over at Gramps and Granny (as I dubbed them), who were still unattended.

Maybe he will get them on the way back, I hoped. And if not our waiter, they can surely send someone else. They are not short-staffed here. I looked around to verify that. Just as I thought, everyone else was being taken care of. What exactly was going on?

While these thoughts were still going through my head, I saw Gramps get up, take his cane, and make his way over to the grill. I could not make out what he said, but from the way he was gesticulating, it seemed he was describing to the chef what he wanted to order. Having finished, he returned to his seat.

Eve was not aware of this whole episode. Now I made her party to my exasperation.

"Why are they giving Gramps the cold shoulder?" I posed.

Eve considered the problem. "Maybe this couple has come here before and ordered so little, the management didn't think it was worth their while to wait on them."

"Eve!"

"Okay, okay. I was just kidding. Of course there's no excuse. A customer is a customer."

"Anyway, there's no sign stating that there is a minimum," I grumbled.

I tried to keep my mind on my meal, but their situation gnawed at me.

Before long, Gramps got up again, returned to the grill, took the plate offered by the chef, and carried it back for his wife. Then he made another trip and brought a portion for himself!

This was too much for me. I can testify from many Thursday nights that no one ever approached the grill. The waiters served everyone. Not only was this irregular, it was downright unfair. "What is going on?" I said, a bit too loud.

Not the reticent type, I told Eve that I could not finish my food until I straightened this out.

Pushing my chair back, I jumped up to look for the owner, Jerry Andrews. As we had become his steady customers, I knew Jerry well. We had developed a nice rapport.

Seeing him at a distance, I made my way in that direction.

"Excuse me, Jerry, I'm sorry to bother you," I began, trying to keep a civil tongue. "See that couple over there?" I pointed accusingly to their table. Jerry's eyes followed my finger. "They were there when we came in. They have been sitting patiently and have not said one word. No waiter has even approached their table. I'm sorry, Jerry, but it hurts me to see people treated like that," I concluded gravely, my tone demanding an answer.

"Mr. Hill," he said to me, obviously taken by the accusation. "I'm more sorry than you."

My eyebrows shot up.

"And believe me, it hurts me more than you," he assured me.

Not a little curious, his enigmatic reply left me hoping Jerry would not leave me hanging. He did not.

"These are my parents." He smiled slightly at my reaction.

"They came in from out of town and agreed to come to dinner on one condition — "

In anticipation, I quickly tried to guess what he was about to say, but my mind drew a blank.

" — that I wouldn't let my staff wait on them. My mother claims that if the waiters serve them, it's taking away time from other customers, and she won't allow me to incur a loss on her account. I've tried to convince her that it's absurd, but my mother stands her ground."

I could see Jerry was feeling bad and was anxious for a chance to explain further. "I know they love coming.

They're so happy to see the business flourishing. But it has to be on their terms."

I walked back to my seat, passing Mr. and Mrs. Andrews on the way. They were both enjoying a portion of chips. They looked up in recognition, nodded politely, and smiled back their gentle smiles.

❧

"What's going on here?" we inquire, utterly astounded.

Even when we try not to sound rude, we are convinced that they have been. On other occasions, we may be baffled, irked, or just plain fed up. Gritting our teeth, we feel our gorge rise.

Until that one piece of information enters onstage, presents itself and takes a bow. We relax, maybe even smile, and then applaud the simplicity of the solution.

13.

That Teacher Is Out of Line

I was there first but, not being the type to start a fight, I let him go ahead of me. Usually someone pushing his way in wouldn't bother me, but now I was in a huge rush, worried about missing my cousin. I had just landed in Florida for my two-week winter vacation. My cousin, who had moved to the south five years before, had invited me to stay with him. My flight had been delayed about an hour. I hoped Morty would still be waiting for me.

When I got outside, the first thing that hit me was the heat. The second thing I noticed was my 6'4" cousin. As soon as he saw me, his pint-size cousin, he ran towards me and almost knocked me over with a bear hug, grabbed my bag, and led me to his car. It was quite a challenge running to keep up with his long strides while at the same time struggling to remove my too heavy sweater.

The first day, Morty fed me well and let me sleep as much as I wanted. Only after that did it become clear that he was fattening me up for the kill. I had gone down there with my own ideas for relaxing, but Morty, it seems, had other plans for me, which he ultimately disclosed.

"The vacation is yours to relax so your heart's content," he said generously. "I'm just asking for a little time for you to tune into your real self." This did not smell good and my senses said, "Beware."

Morty wanted me to sit in on classes with his rabbi. He had been attending these sessions for half a year and claimed they had changed his life.

I tried to put him off, but he held his ground, promising that if I did not like it, he wouldn't push me to continue.

That seemed reasonable. Anyway, I did owe him something for his hospitality. And this was really an easy way to repay him, so why not.

That's how I found myself in an adult education course at the Jewish Studies Center.

At 8:00 sharp, the rabbi swung into action. He was quick, sharp, and very funny. From the first minute, he held us captivated. After an hour I thought he would be talked out, but Rabbi Davis didn't seem to run out of steam.

At 9:00 he opened the floor for discussion. We started firing all kinds of questions at him and at each one, he rose to the challenge and fired back with an amazing insight. He approached every topic with ease, and although we tried, no one could ruffle his feathers.

I confess. I never knew anything about this "rich tradition" he kept quoting, but after only one class he had captured my interest and left me with food for thought.

Admittedly, I was impressed. He had made an impact on me and much to my own surprise, I was willing, even anxious, to come back for more.

When the session was finished, students immediately surrounded the rabbi, continuing to bombard him with questions he seemed to have all the time in the world to answer. I had a few of my own. Morty had to leave, but he suggested that I stay. I stood at the side, watching the animated exchanges until it was my turn.

"Any relative of Morty's is a friend of mine," Rabbi Davis responded to my introduction, pumping my hand enthusiastically and slapping me heartily on the back.

We spoke a little about where I was from and about my background. He commiserated with me about "wasting" my vacation in a classroom, listening to a boring lecture. Was he kidding? This guy seemed like he would not even be boring in his sleep.

I told him that I could easily have sat for another hour, and believe me, very few classes have ever held my attention for two hours straight.

Then we talked about Morty. I mentioned that my cousin was a great admirer of his and had been greatly influenced by the rabbi. He smiled and confirmed, "Yes, he's been coming every week for months." And in the same breath he added, "Tell me, are you also a clown like your cousin? Does it run in the family?"

I responded with a small laugh, but between you and me, I did not think that his question was the least bit funny and it certainly was in poor taste for a teacher.

Granted, Morty has a great sense of humor. But calling him a clown was just not right. Coming from a rabbi, who was supposed to be an educator, it did not sit well with me. Here I am telling him that his student is an admirer of his, and he goes and insults him! That may be okay for us, but for a teacher that's stepping out of line.

My cousin had spoken a lot about this class and his rabbi, how he was an example of blah, blah, blah. Come on, Morty, I thought, you can do better than this.

Deciding that this wasn't for me after all, I cut our conversation short and took my leave, and made my way back to Morty's.

Since some things are better left unsaid, I just told Morty that I had decided that my vacation was for unwinding and not for intellectual pursuits. It was not hard to see that he was disappointed, although it was not me he had to be disappointed in.

The day before I left, the phone rang. Morty was not at home, so I answered it. It was a woman saying she was giving a party for her seven-year-old daughter and wanted to invite Morty. I took down her number. Morty came home soon after, and I was still laughing when I gave him the message.

"How'd you happen to get invited to this big shindig?"

He went over to his desk and pulled out a certificate. It looked like a diploma. My eyes followed the small print.

"We hereby certify that Morton P. Felton has successfully completed an eight-week course in — "

I did a double take.

"Clown School?"

It seems that the rabbi was right. Morty is a clown after all.

❧

The plane took off on its route back north. Morty's cousin peered out the window, watching the trees and houses shrink out of sight, blocked by a cluster of fluffy clouds. The events of the last few days caused him to be struck by the metaphor.

We think we are seeing clearly, but many obstacles cloud our perceptions. Sometimes it is a fragment of missing information whose absence leaves us with an incomplete and therefore unclear — and clearly incorrect — picture.

As the plane lifted and rose above the clouds, Morty's cousin smiled at the allusion.

14.

A Rude Awakening

Shortly after our marriage, my husband and I decided to visit his elderly great-uncle whom I had met once during our engagement. Although he had not been well even then, we heard that, of late, he had taken a turn for the worse.

Auntie Lottie answered the door and immediately told us how happy Uncle Sol would be that we came. She invited us into the sunroom and served us tea and cookies. She wanted to hear all about our wedding which she had not been able to attend, and of course we told her how much both of them had been missed.

Presently, she went to see if Uncle Sol was awake. Returning with a smile and a nod, she motioned for us to follow her.

Great-uncle Sol was lying in his bed, looking more frail than I had remembered him. As weak as he was, his face lit up when he saw Jonathan, his "favorite great-nephew," as he called my husband.

We could sense it was a special moment for him, seeing

us together as a married couple. He questioned us about family, inquired about our parents, and listened intently as we detailed current events and happenings.

Then, after exchanging a few more pleasantries, Uncle Sol lifted himself up slightly.

"Children, how would you like some tips on marriage from an old-timer?" he offered. In those tired eyes there was still a twinkle.

"Of course, Uncle Sol," we chorused.

"When I was young, someone gave me this advice, and I'm passing it on to you. It's saved me from many an argument. For a successful marriage, you need to remember six words."

I was listening. How could I miss this opportunity to learn something so useful?

"The magic formula is — and listen to this carefully. You're right; I'm wrong; I'm sorry."

"But, Uncle Sol," sputtered my husband, "what if I am right? How can I in good conscience say that I'm wrong?"

I stood by his side in complete concurrence.

"You can say you're wrong, when you truthfully think you're right, and still be telling the truth."

"How exactly?" I asked.

"Because you're wrong for arguing, so you *are* wrong, right?"

We laughed together, and I was happier than ever to be part of this wise and wonderful family.

After a while Jonathan decided it was time to leave, apparently not wanting to overtax Uncle Sol. As we stood up, Uncle Sol stated that he wanted to see us to the door. "No, please!" I protested quickly. "We'll see ourselves out. Please don't trouble yourself."

My husband said nothing.

But Uncle Sol was not to be stopped. I watched as this bedridden man attempted to pull himself up. One could see from his facial expressions how much pain every movement caused. I pleaded with this patriarchal personage not to trouble himself, but to no avail. I turned to Jonathan, wordlessly imploring him to tell his uncle to stop. Couldn't he see how difficult it was for him? But my husband stood near Uncle Sol, watching his laborious movements without saying a word.

My eyes filled with tears. *What kind of selfish, unfeeling partner did I get stuck with? Now that we're married he's letting his true colors show. To let this elderly man suffer just for the privilege of being accompanied to the door?!*

Maneuvering himself into a sitting position, Uncle Sol managed to put on his slippers with great effort. Finally, after considerable strain, he stood — somewhat unsteadily at first — on his feet. Inch by inch he shuffled all the way to the front door. Thanking us for our visit, he and Aunt Lottie wished us farewell, and the door closed behind us.

We were standing there together on the stoop, my husband of a month and me. What was there to say? Bitter disappointment engulfed me.

"I see you are upset," my husband began.

I was very impressed with his observation.

"But let me explain. You see, my uncle is in bed all day. You can imagine how detrimental this is to his health. My parents have been saying that the doctors are begging him to get up for a little bit, to walk around — any mild exercise to improve his circulation. Usually he doesn't feel up to it, since it is too painful. When I saw how much he wanted to see us out, I realized this was just the motivation he needed.

"I knew that accompanying us to the door was actually beneficial for him," my compassionate husband concluded, "and that's why I let him do it."

❧

When a person is usually considerate, and has done something out of character, it is more reasonable to consider that he has an explanation unknown to us than to assume that this surprising conduct is the real him.

15.

Apples of Discord

"It certainly is very generous of them," I reasoned, "and I think we should grab the chance."

Yaella, my niece, was being married in Israel, and my brother Danny very much wanted us to be there for the event. Danny's neighbor was traveling and offered to let us use his apartment for a month. My husband was still vacillating.

"It's a perfect setup," my brother encouraged us.

Still, I knew what was on my husband's mind. With a hectic teaching schedule all year, he needed the summer to catch up on his reading and writing, not to mention the preparation for the coming year. Colleagues would certainly need him, and he would have to confer with them from time to time. How could he think of being in Israel, so far away?

Reviewing the pros and cons, the idea of staying in contact by telephone was definitely a deciding factor, but in the last analysis it was the availability of fax and E-mail that finally tipped the scales. We called my brother to tell him we would gratefully take him up on the offer.

I spent my next days shopping and packing, my nights dreaming about a summer in Jerusalem.

It turned out to be an ideal summer for both of us. My husband accomplished everything on his agenda and got to relax a little, too. As soon as we arrived I made a schedule for myself, putting aside time to spend with the family and a slot for touring places I had never seen.

The apartment was centrally located, so people were always dropping by. Maintaining an orderly house and all that it entails proved to be a challenge and filled up a lot of my time, but I still managed to fit in some classes four mornings a week.

Thursday mornings were blocked off for one of my favorite activities — my fruit and vegetable shopping at the open air market in Machaneh Yehudah. From our apartment it was only a short bus ride to the bustling streets where people peddled their wares which varied from season to season. As I crossed the road and entered the marketplace, my eyes darted from one stand to another. They feasted on the displays while I savored a blend of exotic aromas.

A colorful people, I mused, *converging together from every corner of our globe. I am so proud and thankful to be part of them.* My vision was misty as I maneuvered between shopping carts and wagons, weeding my way through baskets and bags brimming with produce. Many were carried by small-framed figures that belied their ability to support such burdens.

Meandering at random from stand to stand, collecting my greens, grains, nuts, and fruits, I stopped a minute to rest. In front of me was a mound of peaches flaunting their giant size and their variegated exterior.

I wasn't sure I could carry much more, but they were irresistible. I grabbed a plastic bag hanging from a hook, took my place beside a little lady who was carefully choosing from the generous heap, and filled up my bag with what I reasoned was a manageable amount.

Wouldn't it be nice to make peach jam, I thought, beginning to have second thoughts about my ambitiousness and ability to lug all this home. That was when I saw a hand reach into my bag and pull out a peach. I turned to see that the hand belonged to the little lady. Flabbergasted, I looked at her with righteous indignation. As I opened my mouth to berate her, I was taken aback by her kind eyes. With a gentle smile she held up the peach she had retrieved from my bag. Rotating the fruit ever so slowly, she revealed to me what I had apparently failed to notice. One side was indeed firm and appealing, but the other side was smashed and spoiled.

How many jams can we avoid by giving people the benefit of the doubt?

16.

A Row in a Boat

We got off to a late start but when we found each other at last, we had a lot more of life behind us than other newlyweds.

Susan and I shared hopes of raising a family. We both opposed the idea of being workaholics. To us it was important to enjoy those years bringing up our children, giving them the best of ourselves.

When the twins were finally born, we kept our promise. Susan gave up her career and became a full-time mom. And me? I get up everyday with the kids at five. I am in my office at 7:30 so that I can leave at 4:30 and be home with enough time to unwind and spend time with the family before we all sit down to supper together.

It is also very important to both of us that bedtime be hassle-free, no tension or tempers allowed. There's no mad rush to put the kids to sleep just so we can get on with other things. The evening is a special time to get to know our children, their doubts and fears, their wishes and dreams, and we treasure those quiet moments together.

With all our good intentions, technology has brought many interferences into that quality time. Cell phones, two-way pagers, E-mail, voice-mail — all those devices are supposed to make us more productive, but in the end, it's easy to become their slave. People have instant access to me, expecting immediate answers from me.

Sometimes I just unplug them all, and sometimes we go out and leave them at home. And two or three times a year we just take a week off and find some quiet place for a family vacation.

Last time we planned a trip, my brother-in-law recommended a small hotel — a four-hour drive from us, where he had previously vacationed. From the way he described it, the place sounded perfect, so we called for reservations.

Good weather makes a good vacation even better. As lovers of the great outdoors, this adage holds particularly true. Each day we try to plan at least one outdoor activity that we can all enjoy. Plans do not always work out as expected, however, and on that particular trip we spent the first two days indoors. On the third day the forecaster's promise of sunny skies materialized, and we were off to Lake Victoria, a spot not far from the hotel, where they rent rowboats, paddleboats, and canoes, by the hour. The early bird catches the worm, and we were the first to arrive... with an oversized can.

Our third-grade twin daughters, Faith and Hope — we get a lot of comments on our choice of names, but believe me, that is what pulled us through when our long-awaited daughters were still a dream — chose the canoe. Susan strapped them into the life preservers and pushed off from the dock. I climbed into a rowboat along with our son Seth, born two years after the twins.

We later traded seats, so Seth could take the oars. He was a little inexperienced, but caught on in no time and was soon having a blast. We talked, we laughed, threw some water on each other, did a little fishing, and spent some good quality time together. I did not forget to send up a thank you to the One who blessed me with this day.

I do not know how they found their way into our sunny day, but when I looked up, a scattering of unfriendly clouds had appeared. I was hopeful that my son and I would still get in some more of that private time, despite the change in weather.

Sooner than we wished, however, the air started to feel damp. The sky was darkening by the minute, and before long the drops started falling. I did not want to take a chance at being caught in a downpour and so I figured we should head back. Seth was not the least bit concerned and begged for more time. I wanted to be on his side, but someone here had to be levelheaded.

We were about fifteen minutes from shore. I took the

oars from Seth, who was not overly keen about relinquishing them, and dug them deep into the water. The rain was coming down harder now. I tried to pick up speed.

Meanwhile, Seth, who had been sitting behind me, inched forward and threw himself on me, grasping tightly onto my shoulders.

What father does not wait for such a hug, that warm, spontaneous show of affection? At any other time my response would have been euphoric. But even good things can be poorly timed. And just then I could not appreciate it. He was simply in my way.

"Seth, sit down please," I encouraged him.

"It's OK, Dad." And he hugged harder.

I tried to row anyway, but could not get the proper leverage with him hanging on me, and I was getting annoyed. The rain was becoming stronger, and my patience weaker. Not known for my forbearance, I do make an extra effort to keep my short fuse in check with my family.

Why botch it after such a nice day? I reasoned with myself. Isn't this the kind of experience you long for?

I tried to gently shake him off, but Seth, a child not always big on hugs, clung to me.

Finally, I exploded.

"Will you get off me already!" I thundered. "How many times do I have to tell you! You're bothering me!"

"Sorry Dad," he apologized in a little voice as he unfolded his arms. "I just wanted to — "

There was a catch in his voice. Then I heard the hurt.

"I was just trying to cover you, so you wouldn't get so wet."

You might argue that the father did not misjudge his son. He knew he meant well. But, unwittingly he did, because actually his son meant even better.

17.

The Little Boring Speaker

My brother Eli and his wife Nina were making their first bar mitzvah. Anyone who has ever arranged such an occasion can tell you how much planning goes into that milestone.

The bigger hall or the closer one? Do we invite second cousins? What color should we make the invitations? How many guests should we plan on? Where do we find a patient and competent teacher for bar mitzvah lessons?

My brother and sister-in-law made it through all the preparations, and we made it too — we were all there. Our parents, all the sisters and brothers and their families, aunts, uncles, friends, neighbors, and second cousins, celebrating together with Nina and Eli.

And there was Ari, the bar mitzvah boy, looking so grown-up in his new suit. All the months of practicing paid off — he read the Torah without one mistake.

We were sitting and listening to Ari deliver his bar mitzvah speech. It was longer than the usual speech of a young and inexperienced speaker, and we sat marveling at how well he held the attention of his audience, amazed at his clear and well-organized presentation.

This euphoric state was quickly shattered as one of Eli's neighbors turned around and whispered to me, "He's a boring speaker."

Just like that! Straight to my face! Hard to believe, right? And that's not all. From the look on his face it even seemed as if he were expecting me to agree with his evaluation of my nephew!

I glared at him. How could a guest make such a callous statement to a family member — even if it were true? We all remember what our first-grade teachers taught us, "If you have nothing good to say, say nothing at all." It's hard to believe that a normal adult would do something like that.

Do you think I could enjoy the rest of that speech? I was just glad that I was the one who heard it and not anyone else. And mostly I was glad that my brother was spared. Eli was sitting too far away to overhear anything, and besides, he was too busy listening to Ari.

How do you deal with such thoughtlessness? I was thinking when this neighbor turned to me again and said, with the same conviction as before:

"Take it from me. I've heard a lot of bar mitzvah boys, and I'm telling you again, this one is a born speaker."

❧

Off by one syllable. But look how far off those extra two letters took him.

Verbal misunderstandings are so often the reason for dark suspicion, long-lasting grudges, and even nasty feuds. Nonetheless, we continue to trust our ears, rarely questioning their infallibility, even though they fool us time and again.

Of course, we human beings were created to be dependent on our senses, and surely our auditory perception, which helps us acquire essential knowledge about the world around us. At the same time, to help safeguard us against the hazards of miscommunication, the Almighty has warned us to take caution. The precept of judging favorably teaches us that when our senses bring us a denunciatory verdict, we should contest the validity of this testimony.

18.

Now You See It, Now You Don't

S omeone had to volunteer for the job, and I seemed to be the most likely candidate. Actively involved in our town's well-attended lecture series, I took on the responsibility of posting the publicity in my area. One of the most frustrating parts of this weekly ritual is that the announcement flyers are often removed or covered over. It is not unusual to pass a notice board where two hours earlier I had put up a poster to see it removed and replaced with one advertising a computer for sale. My immediate reaction is to rip down the computer advertisement and put my sign back up. After all, mine was up there first.

Then my cerebral center takes charge and tells me that perhaps the person selling his computer did not pull down my sign at all. Maybe the tack became loose and the notice fell off or the wind blew it away — and he came in all innocence and found an empty space. So I leave his ad alone and find somewhere else to put mine.

Just recently I caught someone red-handed, putting up a sign on a bulletin board and obscuring six other notices.

There's no denying it this time, I thought with conviction. *He's not going to get away with it. Someone's got to set this guy straight. Doesn't he realize that he's depriving other people of the chance to sell their goods?*

I approached him and let him have it. He heard me out. When I finally finished my tirade, he looked me straight in the eye.

"This is not my notice. I took it down for a minute to photocopy some information. I'm just putting it back where I found it," his voice trailed off, as he turned on his heel and walked away.

❧

But what about the person who put it there in the first place? What did he have in mind when he covered up the other signs? We cannot know for sure, but there is a chance that he also had a perfectly acceptable reason for what he did. He just deserves the chance to explain himself.

19.

Three's a Crowd

The volume of boisterous voices escalated steadily, as story after story whizzed around the room.

"Like when we went out to eat and all got food poisoning." That was Jenny, who groaned and clutched at her stomach as if that agonizing pain had suddenly reappeared.

"I still can't forget when Shira broke her leg." That was Dahlia from her place near the closet. "I just freaked when I saw her falling."

"Those were nothing compared to when Shira fell out of the boat." That was Lisa. "I thought I'd die."

"You thought *you* would die?" put in Shira, remembering her one attempt at canoeing. "Speaking of water, remember when the neighbor walked into the middle of our water fight to tell us to be quiet and walked out drenched?" The room exploded with laughter, as memories floated by.

"Do you remember when Cindy told us she was engaged? Wasn't it amazing she managed to keep such a secret from us?"

"Or when we stayed up so late cramming for mid-terms that we slept through the exam the next day"

It was the beginning of May. We were reminiscing, recalling some of the highlights of the past year, the sweet times as well as the tougher moments. We philosophized, we analyzed — contemplating the many problems and pitfalls of dorm life. We concluded that many of the arguments — and some of them were quite heated — were sparked by simple misunderstandings.

"If you're talking about misjudgments, I've got a story for you, girls."

We all looked up to see our dorm counselor adviser, Ariella, standing in the doorway. She accepted our invitation to join us and plopped herself down on a bed. A tried and proven tale-spinner, our dear Ariella knew she had a captive audience.

"I realize it could never have the same impact on you as it had on me," she smiled reflectively. "Hearing a story can never compete with actually experiencing it." We nodded understandingly and encouraged her to go on with what was sure to be a "good one."

"I thought I knew what was happening, and yet I completely misread the whole situation." She seemed to be talking more to herself than to us, but then she picked up her head and continued with her usual gusto.

"This all happened when I was a student. I shared a room in a dorm with two other girls. As we all know, it does not always work out, especially a threesome, but this time it really clicked.

"We were in the middle of exams. I had spent the evening in the study hall, having foolishly left the bulk of review for the last minute. It was late at night when I finally walked into the room and saw my roommates, Rebecca and Ella, talking excitedly. As soon as they saw me, they stopped short. Obviously, they had not counted on me walking in just then. I was sorry I had not given them more time to finish sharing their little secret.

"You girls know how it is. You walk into a room, and everyone is talking, and then they suddenly stop, so you have the distinct feeling that they were talking about you.

"Since everything had been going so nicely between us until then, I was totally unprepared for this. I only hoped it was not going to be a major clash. Dumping my stuff on the bed, I went out to wash my face and get ready for bed. A few minutes later I came back. Approaching our room, I could hear some kind of commotion and then my roommates' laughter. *Pretty funny when you're on the inside,* I thought cheerlessly. I stood outside a few seconds more and then turned the knob quietly. Ella and Rebecca were standing in the middle of the room in animated conversation. My instinctive reaction was to take the broom Ella was holding and use it on my two snob-bish roommates.

"You can be sure I avoided looking at them and went straight to bed. That night I put the pillow over my head and quietly cried myself to sleep.

"The next morning I awoke in a sun-flooded room. The first thing I heard was Rebecca whispering to Ella, and I reluctantly realized that eventually I would have to face that cliquey twosome.

"As soon as they saw me turn over, Ella called out to Rebecca, 'OK, now you can tell her.'

"'No, you tell her, Ella. You were the one who came to the rescue.'

"'*What are they talking about?* I thought apprehensive-ly, still not willing to come out from under the security of my blanket.

"'You don't know what we saved you from,' Ella grinned as she walked towards my bed.

"'What do you mean?' I asked, finally showing my face.

"'I'm sure it was poisonous. It had at least twenty legs and five pairs of wings,' winced Rebecca, always one to exaggerate any number.

"'Totally grotesque,' confirmed Ella, rolling her eyes melodramatically. 'We know how petrified you are of those things. Aren't you glad we didn't tell you about it?!'

"'You cannot fathom what we went through last night,'

Rebecca called over her shoulder, reaching for the broom and raising it theatrically. 'Armed to the teeth in battle array' she smartly adjusted the collar of her robe, 'with a cry of *"guerre a mort"* on our lips, we declared war. Sword in hand 'she swung the broom in front of me, 'we charged fearlessly into battle against the formidable foe,' ended Rebecca, heroically whacking the broom at the end of the bed and concluding her performance with a low bow.

"'You would have been totally hysterical,' giggled Ella. But don't worry, we got rid of it as quietly as we could, while you were sleeping. We must have spent half an hour chasing that thing around the room, finally smashing it with the broom, just missing your head by a few inches.'"

❧

Why don't people speak up, explain themselves, and save us all the aggravation? We give them favorable judgment by understanding that they assessed the situation and concluded that telling us would cause more aggravation than not telling. They know that we'll eventually find out and forgive them.

Would we choose to do it that way? Not necessarily. But our task is to focus on the fact that they have good intentions, and even our benefit in mind.

20.

Where's Mama?

The first time I met Ruth Klein-Berg was at a conference where I heard her speak. Her well-disguised European accent aroused my interest. Being a public speaker myself, I was impressed and curious to know more about her. I found out she was a successful trial attorney at a prestigious law firm in the Midwest. Later, at the dinner reception, I happened to notice Ruth reach for a drink. When a tattoo peeked out of her sleeve, I was aghast. On a classy lady like this! What kind of tattoo would she possibly want? I put my glasses on to get a better view. I was shocked. This was no tattoo, this was a row of numbers.

As a child of survivors, I grew up feeling — different. I felt that if I could just grasp my parents' war experience, I would better understand them and through them, myself. My mother always told me it was impossible for anyone who was not there to "know." The need to relate to that point grew stronger as I grew older. I instinctively gravitated towards war victims, hoping they could give me some of the insights I so desperately needed.

Once I saw those numbers, my initial fascination with Ruth intensified. Being drawn by her personality and mode of expression, I felt Ruth's story held answers for me. I took a chance and introduced myself. We hit it off right away. Over the years I have gotten to know this strong and brave woman, and we have become friends. She has shared her incredible life story with me. The following is a key piece of that story.

I was the youngest child of a traditional, well-to-do Jewish family in Poland. I had two sisters and a brother, all considerably older. My oldest sister was married and expecting her first child.

Rumors of a German invasion were growing. My father, David Klein, was a well-respected doctor. He had many friends and connections who helped him send my siblings away to safety, even my married sister and her husband. My father felt I was too young to join them in their escape, which would involve constant running and hiding, so he paid a hefty sum of money for me to be hidden with a local gentile family, in the hope that somehow I would be saved. The Germans invaded; Poland fell quickly, and many thousands were arrested, including my dear father. Neighbors betrayed my host family, and my hiding place was disclosed. As an 11-year-old child, I was sent to Birkenau.

Through countless miracles, I somehow survived. I'm sure those miracles were connected to my parents' prayers.

After liberation, I wandered from place to place looking for food and shelter, hoping to find anyone who would help me. I was all of 16 years old.

I was always searching for a familiar face. One day, while lingering on a vacant bench, I spotted Itzig Fisher, our baker, a *lantzleit* (fellow townsperson). I begged him for any news he had regarding the whereabouts of my relatives. It was he who informed me that my father was no longer alive. Papa had been shot at police headquarters. As painful as that news was, knowing that my dear father had been spared the concentration camp was some kind of inner consolation. I wanted to ask about my mother, my sisters, and my brother, but I knew in my heart that he would have told me, had he known. I eventually had to accept that they had probably perished like all the others.

Are there words to express how I felt, how we all felt as the truth became clear? I was filled with indescribable grief, and I drained myself of tears.

Two days later, at this low point, I met a woman I recognized, who told me she had seen my mother about seventy kilometers from where we were standing. I had been too afraid to feel or hope. Now, the idea of finding my mother spurred me on, filling me with a strength I believed I would never have again.

A month passed. After running from place to place, hanging onto any lead, piecing together any information, I found my mother.

The woman I found was, indeed, my mother; yet she was not Mama. Her personality had completely changed. Mama was not Mama. She was withdrawn. She showed no signs of happiness in seeing me. She would hardly look at me, although I was certain she knew who I was.

"Mama," I cried, "what will be?"

She stared at me blankly, and I heard those words that have replayed in my ears thousands of times since then: "I don't know what will be. I can't take care of myself, and I can't take care of you."

I was choking. I could barely breathe.

"Mama," I begged. "Mama!"

She mumbled something about Papa always taking care of everything, knowing what to do. Of course, Mama had been so dependent on Papa, who directed our lives and was in charge of everything. Even in good times, Mama was at a loss without him. I gazed with a broken heart at my dear Mama, who had once been so loving, full of life and fun. The war had destroyed her.

After Birkenau, I comforted myself that nothing could ever hurt me again. Nothing could get worse. Now I experienced a new horror. I was an orphan with a living mother who was not really alive.

I do not know how I survived that meeting.

Somehow, with G-d's help, relatives in America found me. They sent affidavits, visas, everything I needed. They were very good to me. Despite their own unstable financial situation, they took me in as one of their children and provided me with all my needs. With time, their nurturing enabled me to begin life anew.

I poured all my strength into learning English, obtaining a high school equivalency diploma, and getting into a decent college. Scholarships, and night and summer jobs, paid the bills. I was accepted into a prestigious law school. That's when I met my husband. Michael had just finished his medical residency. He wanted to get married as soon as possible. But I did not feel normal enough to get married. Lucky for me, Michael was very confident. He dragged me to the *chuppah*. Thank G-d, today we have a good life and four wonderful children.

When the kids were young, they would ask if they had grandparents like their friends. I was unable to cope with the whole thing and somehow ignored the questions. When my oldest was five, he came upon my only picture of Mama.

"Who's this?"

I evaded the question and changed the subject. But it make me think, and I knew I just could not continue making believe my mother did not exist. My heart was breaking. After four or five tearful, sleepless nights, Michael convinced me that together we should visit my mother. I had known for some time that she was living in Canada, supporting herself as a seamstress.

We arrived unannounced. We did not want to risk rejection. What do you say to your mother you have not seen in ages?

"Mama, this is my husband, Dr. Michael Berg."

I think Mama fell for his charm and the doctor thing. By the end of the visit, she actually smiled. But Mama was not ready for more.

For years after, I made up stories for the kids to explain why Bubby never visited and why we could not visit her. I forged birthday cards to protect them. In reality, I was protecting myself from something I could not understand or accept.

During those years I called Canada at infrequent intervals. Somewhere along the line, my mother expressed interest in meeting my children. Perhaps Mama did not feel burdened by them now that they were almost adults?

The family was thrilled at the prospect of gaining a grandmother. Mama showed some signs of affection but still did not want to be involved in their lives. Meanwhile, I still ached. I was happy that my children, in some small way, had a Bubby, but could I say I had a mother?

One night I was driving home from work. I turned on the radio. A program was already in progress. Some woman called in describing her daily battle with a debilitating disease. She described very intense feelings of inadequacy in filling her role as wife and mother. Her teenage daughter was very ashamed that she was showing signs of her weakening condition. Her youngest son, age eight, was being cheated out of having a "real" mother. She described her depression, her frustration over responsibilities that completely overwhelmed her.

She then spoke about the conflict she faced in becoming a grandmother. She had always dreamed about grandchildren, and now she could barely hold the baby. She had so looked forward to being a very involved grandma, shopping for all those adorable things, babysitting. Now the birth of each additional grandchild meant failure. She felt as if she had let down her daughter, her oldest, with whom she had always been so close. Her new grandson evoked feelings of resentment, and his very existence screamed, "You are incapable, deficient — wanting, wanting, wanting."

She wished everyone and anything that aroused those feelings of inadequacy would disappear and with them her guilt for feeling that way.

I almost crashed the car. Pulling over to the side of the road, hardly able to shut the ignition, the tears blinding my sight, I sobbed for what seemed like hours. I called my husband and asked him to come and get me — I could not drive, I could not even talk.

Later that night I finally could speak about what had

happened. I told Michael how this woman, a stranger on the radio, had helped me to understand my mother. Here was a woman who not only could not enjoy her new grandchild, she confessed that she actually wished the baby had never been born. Her perception of herself, through him, as incapable, robbed her of all her potential joy and left her guilt-ridden.

For the first time since seeing my mother after the war, I began to understand. Mama had been a super *balabuste,* a warm and completely dedicated mother and wife. The war had destroyed all of that. Mama could not cope with those losses. Nor could she cope with what remained. She did not have the strength to care for me, and she could not bear to be a different kind of mother, one who could not give.

"I wished," the voice on the radio re-echoed in my ears, "everyone and anything that evoked those feelings of inadequacy would disappear."

I felt a tremendous need to see Mama as soon as possible. Although I was in over my head at work, I made plans to visit her two weeks later.

A few days after hearing that radio show, I was sitting in a meeting with judges, where there are no interruptions. To my surprise, a phone was brought to me. It was my oldest son, David.

"Mom, Bubby had a stroke. She's in intensive care. Get here as soon as possible."

I felt the war again, the bombs, the losses, the fear. I got up, told my colleagues I had a family emergency. Landing in Canada six hours later, I just hoped it was not too late.

I'll never stop thanking G-d for allowing me to find her alive and conscious. All the years I had been afraid to even touch Mama. Now I cradled her head in my arms. Her eyes were filled with tears.

"It's OK, Mama. I know you love me. I know you always loved me."

She squeezed my hand with what seemed to be her last ounce of strength. She motioned for me to lower my head, as if she wanted to tell me something. I bent my head to her face, and she kissed me for the first time in forty-four years. We held hands and cried. There were no words, everything was understood. Fifteen minutes later my mother passed away.

❧

No doubt we can find it in our hearts to forgive the most difficult of personalities, if we know they had suffered the terror of World War II.

Sad to say, there are different kinds of wars. People have their own private war stories filled with much loss and pain. There are even psychological concentration camps, where the victim and the tormentors are very real. Such victims, in spite of the difficulties they present us, deserve our forbearance, sympathetic regard, and most certainly our forgiveness.

But where are their branded numbers to warn us that they have come from a place of suffering?

The Almighty has commanded us to judge our fellow person with favor, with generosity, with humility. Just because there is so much about people we will never know.

21.

That's the Way the Cookie Crumbles

This story has been circulating for some time.
Somebody has finally put it to rhyme.

Several long hours before her flight
A woman waited at the airport one night.

She found a book in the airport shop
And a bag of cookies, and a place to drop.

So engrossed in her book, yet she happened to see
The man sitting by her, as bold as could be,

Take a cookie or two from the bag in between
(which she tried to ignore to avoid a big scene).

So she munched the cookies and watched the clock,
As the bold cookie thief diminished her stock.

She thought, more irate as the minutes ticked by,
"If I weren't so nice, I'd blacken his eye."

With each cookie *she* took, *he* took one too.
There was only one left — what should she do?

With a smile on his face, and a nervous laugh,
He took the last cookie and broke it in half.

He offered her half as he ate the other.
She snatched it from him, and muttered, "Oh! Brother!

This guy has some nerve! He's totally rude!
Why doesn't he show some gratitude!!"

She had never before in her life been so galled.
She sighed with relief when her flight was soon called.

She gathered her things and walked to the gate,
Without looking back at the thieving ingrate.

She boarded the plane, sank into her seat,
And looked for her book, which was almost complete.

As she reached in her handbag, she spied with surprise
Her *own* bag of cookies in front of her eyes!

"If mine are here," she moaned in despair,
"the others were *his,* and *he* tried to share."

Too late to apologize, she realized with grief
That she was the rude one, the ingrate, the thief.

How many times have we "known" we were right,
Only to find we were on the wrong flight.

22.

She Loves Me, She Loves Me Not

"A great big mazal tov, Gila!"

"We are so happy for you, darling. You certainly deserve the best."

"When was it official?"

"We heard he's a wonderful boy…"

The phone did not stop ringing. It seemed all my friends, relatives, and neighbors were as happy as I. And the good wishes kept coming.

Perhaps because I was the first child in my family to be married, or maybe because we're a very close-knit community. Or was it that I'm the last one in my class to get engaged? Whatever it was, one thing was for sure, I was getting the royal treatment and loving every minute of it.

All of a sudden there was so much to plan, a million details to arrange. But first things first, and that was the engagement party. We talked about having it in a hall; however, I had always dreamed about having my engagement party on our landscaped lawn. In the end everyone agreed.

We had a week to arrange everything. There were lights to be strung, tables and chairs to be rented, plates, platters, and cutlery to consider, and a menu to plan, and that was just the tip of the iceberg. A bit overwhelmed, we relaxed a little when my mother's best friend, an amateur party planner, offered her help. She began by suggesting that we hire a tent — just in case.

The party was called for a Wednesday night. On Monday, a pageant of culinary delights began filing in. The first to arrive was a Viennese torte impressively balanced on the right hand of my Aunt Sarah, who was simultaneously planting kisses on everyone in sight. After that, a tray of dreamy pastries — neat rows of tiny fruit tarts, picture-perfect petit fours, miniature eclairs, and Napoleons — showed up, courtesy of our next-door neighbor.

Early Tuesday morning Aunt Shayna dropped by and handed us her famous streusel kuchen. She caught us in our robes, but we were not too sleepy to admire her creation. My aunt was followed by cousin Tova, who ceremoniously presented us with a chocolate trifle in a tall crystal bowl.

My father's partner's wife sent over a fruit platter, heaped high with a rainbow of delectable fruits. The colors were sensational, and we all concurred that it would be a perfect centerpiece.

My younger sister, who borrowed a neighbor's kitchen in

order to surprise me, presented me with a frosted layer cake. "Best catch of the year" was lettered across the top. Considering we had shared a room for all these years, I thought that was generous of her. (On second thought, was she referring to me, or was it he she meant?)

And then Bubby, my dear sweet Bubby, added to this procession of tempting creations a basket of her own mouthwatering assorted cookies. We detected oatmeal bars, gingersnaps, coconut kisses, and caramel chews, not to mention the mandelbrodt, made with all the love only a grandmother can give.

On Wednesday morning two friends appeared at the door supporting a cake made in the shape of a house, formed from cookie wafers, candies, lollipops, jellybeans, and licorice. On the "door" was written "Gila and David Kramer."

The *piece de resistance* came late Wednesday afternoon from my best friend. Covered with snowy white icing, it was a work of art and architecture, a multi-tiered masterpiece, decorated with lifelike, edible "daisies" and "chrysanthemums" on a background of picot lace and trimmed with a lush border of piped green "leaves." An attached note read, "Dear Gila, Lavished with love, Aviva."

Somewhere in between came a white chocolate horn filled with chocolate dipped strawberries, and a mocha cream roll, but I can't remember exactly when, and I am not even certain from whom.

And the flowers! Oh, what flowers! The arrangements were adorned with curled ribbons and bows and all the beautiful wishes for David and me. As the house filled with all the floral fragrances mixed with the tantalizing smells of the baked goods, I thought to myself, is all of this just for me? I felt like a real princess.

The party was called for 7:30, but we ended up being ready much earlier. So organized, we even had a chance to nap and were calm and relaxed when the first guest arrived.

My new in-laws, ever prompt, were on the button. They walked in at 7:30, followed by David, his two brothers and his sister. After greetings and good wishes were exchanged, I brought them into the living room where all the flowers were displayed, assuring them that I was overwhelmed with what they had sent.

"Which one is from us?" David's mother asked curiously. Of course, how could she know, I smiled, the room is full of so many bouquets and gorgeous arrangements. Taking her hand, I led her towards the piano. "This one is from David," I pointed to the long-stemmed pink roses, "and this one," I pointed to the biggest and most elaborate flowers in the room, "is from you!" Squeezing her hand, I kissed my mother-in-law-to-be on the cheek, knowing she would be pleased that I appreciated her generosity.

She let go of my hand and seemed to move away a bit. "I don't understand," she said, clearly disturbed. "I warned the florist not to make it big. I definitely didn't want such a large arrangement. Right?" she turned to Mr. Kramer, "we didn't want anything that big?" Mr. Kramer nodded emphatically.

Why are you saying this? I thought, deeply offended. *Is that the way you want to start off this relationship? Even if you feel that way, even if you didn't want to spend so much money on me. Why tell me now,* I thought resentfully, *and spoil this evening after we worked so hard to make it memorable? Accept the mistake graciously and let me think you really cared about me that much.* At that moment I felt I had been suddenly dethroned.

At least I had enough good sense not to start up with a newly acquired mother-in-law, and I kept my mouth shut. I looked towards David, hoping for some sympathy, but his mind seemed to be elsewhere. I was not sure he even heard his mother's complaint against the florist.

Not knowing what the next move should be or who should make it, my eyes searched desperately for my mother.

I guess a mother's and daughter's heartstrings are tied tight, because who do you think walked in just then? There she was, with her warm, reassuring smile. I quickly made my way over to her.

Meanwhile, Mrs. Kramer turned to her son, and I overheard her say, "David, I'm sorry. I warned the store not to make my arrangement *too* large. I wanted to send something very lovely for Gila, but I was concerned that it shouldn't be too big — after all, how does it look if my flowers are bigger than yours!"

Taking a deep breath and lifting my shoulders back up, I hurried over to David's mother. I gave her the third kiss of the evening, absolutely thrilled (and utterly relieved) that I was lucky enough to be getting such a kind and sensitive new "Mom."

❧

It was the first close run-in, but chances are, not the last.

When we acquire new family, we must know that each family has its own ways, mannerisms, customs, and habits. We are inevitably presented with the need to develop skills of patience and understanding to successfully deal with the challenges of family life.

When we feel our new relatives, or our old ones for that matter, have acted offensively, it is important to be mindful of this often overlooked fact: There is a second side to every story. We are on the road to judging others favorably when we have the desire to find out what that other side might be.

23.

Something Else Cooking

The setting: The kosher kitchen of a large educational institution. The new assistant principal, Mr. Lewis, was in the kitchen on an errand. Before leaving, he scanned the well-organized operation. Impressive as it was, something was amiss. Serving several hundred students, it was equipped with only one stove. Surely the standards of kashrus would require having separate stoves for meat and dairy. He mulled over the idea for a few days, not wanting to make an impetuous move. But the more he thought about it, the more he was convinced that he had the right idea.

Mr. Lewis approached the chef, "Uncle Ben," with his suggestion. It was quickly vetoed.

"I've run this kitchen since you were in knickers, and we don't need any advice!" replied Uncle Ben with an impatient wave of his hand.

Undaunted, Mr. Lewis persisted. "Of course you're more experienced than I am in the kitchen, Uncle Ben. But considering the size of this institution, it just seems reasonable to have another stove."

"Nope," repeated Uncle Ben. "No need for it," he stated with definite finality.

Convinced that he could eventually win over the chef if he went about it in a different way, Mr. Lewis presented his idea to the principal.

"We have no funds in the budget for it," said the principal. "But if you feel it is important and can work out the details, I have no objection to you donating one."

The next day Mr. Lewis bought a stovetop and a table and installed them in the kitchen.

Uncle Ben listened silently as the assistant principal explained that he had the principal's approval. With an encouraging smile, Mr. Lewis added, "I hope this stove will prove helpful."

Later in the day, the assistant principal popped in to check on the new arrangement. He could not believe his eyes. The table was knocked over, and the stove lay on the floor.

The nerve of that Uncle Ben! Imagine knocking over a new stove like that!

Mr. Lewis picked up the table, stood it upright and put the stove back on it. He hurried off to a meeting, all the while muttering under his breath. Later he returned to look for Uncle Ben. To his utter amazement, he saw that the table was again knocked over and the stove was on the floor.

That guy is wild! Completely out of control.

He bent to pick up the table and noticed that the stove-top had several dents in it. "From two good pushes," said Mr. Lewis with clenched teeth.

Just then the door opened, and a kitchen worker walked in. "Thanks for the new stove, Mr. Lewis. It was a good idea. Even Uncle Ben liked it. We'll need to replace that table, though. It only stands for a short while, and then it buckles under. Must be a defective leg...."

Even when the evidence weighs against a person, judging favorably means considering other options. You never know when there might be... something else cooking.

24.

Plain Turbulence

The convention was scheduled for mid-winter. My cousin Abie Rosen was preparing and presenting a paper at an international conference in London. His wife, Fay, was coming along for a vacation, of sorts. For lack of a suitable alternative, they were bringing along their 22-month-old Davie and their infant.

Before their scheduled flight to England, they had requested and had subsequently confirmed that they would be given bulkhead seats with a bassinet. Those seats would also provide extra floor space where their toddler could stretch out.

As it turned out, not only were the bulkhead seats not available, but there was a major complication with the seating, requiring Abie and Fay to sit separately. In practical terms this meant that for seven hours both parents would have to hold the children, since the area by their feet was not spacious enough for little Davie. Despite extensive negotiations, the distraught crewmembers could not help them. Had Fay or Abie known what was in store for them, they never would have agreed. Unaided by foresight, they resigned themselves to the apparently unalterable conditions.

The flight was even worse than they could have anticipated. Finally landing in Heathrow Airport, they descended from the airplane, sore, stiff, and completely drained.

Needless to say, a few days before their return, they contacted the airline and even went to the office in person, to confirm that they would be provided with a bassinet on their return flight. They spoke to the supervisor, wrote down the name and position of anyone promising to fulfill their request, and had it all triple-checked on the computer. Just no repeat performance, they begged.

That morning Abie placed one last confirmation call before the taxi picked them up for the airport.

Boarding the plane, they made their way to their assigned bulkhead seats. As they arranged their packages in the overhead compartment, they delightedly noted the plentiful floor space for the things they needed to keep handy for Davie.

When the seatbelt sign went off, the stewardess brought the bassinet which would be affixed to the wall in front of them. But, lo and behold, the bassinet refused to attach to the screws. No matter how hard the stewardess or Abie tried, it simply would not adhere to the wall.

Dismal memories of their recent flight danced in front of

Fay. She hugged the baby tighter.

The stewardess pleasantly suggested placing the bassinet on the floor. But where would Davie sleep? On her lap again? Fay started to panic and insisted they be let off the plane.

Fay's problematic demand brought a flight attendant on the scene with his own solution: why not switch seats with the two people in the adjoining seats? Those seats also had the appropriate screws in front of them to attach a bassinet.

"Maybe they won't mind," the stewardess coaxed. Abie generally felt it unfair to put people on the spot like that. But this time, he was at that point of desperation where principles could be set aside.

"No, we want to sit right where we are," said the closer of the two ladies, and continued reading her magazine.

Fay's hopes for a semi-normal flight crumbled.

"What a selfish lady," Fay thought resentfully and voiced her opinion to Abie. He readily agreed and added a comment about living in a world devoid of compassion.

"Some people only look out for themselves!" Abie declared emphatically, making sure the uncooperative party could hear every word.

Meanwhile, more of the cabin crew appeared, each one making an attempt to force the bassinet into place. Switching seats must have seemed the logical solution, because someone else made the same suggestion, pointing to the two women next to them. Fay explained that the people were not willing to accommodate and refused to budge.

At that point the woman unobtrusively put down her magazine. From her troubled expression it was evident that the Rosens' words had hit their mark. Her eyes scanned the assemblage, some of whom were fiddling unsuccessfully with the bassinet, while the rest deliberated equally unproductively on the side.

"Excuse me," she interrupted. "Please understand," came the words of gentle protest. "I'm not stubborn, and I don't want to be difficult." She motioned towards the adjacent seat, at the young woman reclining with her eyes closed, whom the Rosens had not noticed until then. The mother caressed her daughter's hand endearingly. "My daughter is ill," she concluded bleakly. "I'm taking her to Boston for treatments. A moment ago she told me she was in pain. I'm sure you understand that just now I'd rather move her as little as possible."

In the middle of all this, someone somehow managed to attach the bassinet.

The children fell asleep, leaving Fay both with time to get to know her seatmate, a kind and caring woman, and with the desire to develop more of a talent for giving people the benefit of the doubt.

❧

Over the years we have received many stories about people who stubbornly refused to give up their seats, even upon request. From the surprise outcomes we understand that there are many valid reasons that people cannot move.

When others do not come through for us in our time of need, we are undeniably frustrated or even angry. While we may, and often must, ask for help, we must also brace ourselves for refusal. But how do we come to terms with this rebuff? By acknowledging that we can never really know the hardships involved in complying with our request.

25.
Whodunit?

My son Simon was engaged to be married, and the time had come to buy a diamond ring for his future wife. Simon's grandmother, who lives in South Africa, offered to give us a stone.

Grandma called us and said, "Children, many years ago I received an expensive pair of diamond earrings as a gift from my sister-in-law. Each stone weighs about a karat. I'm sending you one to have for Simon's bride. I want it to be a family heirloom."

We were very touched by her generosity. Shortly after, the stone was sent to us with a close friend of Grandma's, and I picked it up from the friend's home. Now I had to take it to my jeweler to have it set.

I went with my daughter-in-law-to-be so that it would be the ring of her choice. She admired the stone, as did the jeweler, and picked out a pretty setting. The jeweler said he would keep the stone in his safe overnight and bring it to a setter in the morning. He said I could come back for it anytime after 11:00.

I thoroughly trusted the jeweler. He was a man with an excellent reputation, and I had always been pleased with his service in the past. We are also distant relatives. I confidently left the diamond and went home.

The next day, I came back to pick up the ring. The jeweler took me aside and said, "There's something you should know. That diamond is a fake."

I almost fainted. It was impossible.

Still in shock, I asked the jeweler, "How do you know?"

He said, "I suspected something when you brought it in, because it looked too bright and clean to be real. A diamond that size, with no imperfection, would cost a fortune! I didn't want to say anything to you yesterday, however, until I got another opinion, so later I asked the setter with whom I've worked a long time.

"I didn't tell him of my suspicion. I wanted an unbiased opinion, so I simply asked, "How much do you think this stone is worth?'

" 'Worth? Are you kidding? This is a fake!'"

The jeweler continued, "I didn't know if I should tell you at all, but I thought that if your daughter-in-law would one day find out that it's not real, she would think you had purposely led her to believe otherwise. It could be a sticky situation."

I was still in a daze, but composed myself enough to ask, "Was the diamond in your sight the entire time the setting was done?"

"Yes," the jeweler assured me.

"Did the setter take it into a back room?" I pursued.

"No," he answered definitively.

I was at a loss. All I knew was that I was out of a diamond and not sure why!

The jeweler saw how upset I was and said, "I have a diamond expert coming in this afternoon. Do you want him to check the stone?"

I did not think I had anything to gain, so I declined his offer.

I went home and told my husband the whole horrific story. His eyes opened wide as I said the word "fake" and stayed that way until I finished the story. We sat together in silence.

"Now, let's take it slow and not jump to any conclusions," my husband said at last. "We don't want to fall into the trap of suspecting innocent people, do we? Let's go over the facts again," he suggested. "How well do we know this jeweler?"

"You remember him," I said. "We've dealt with him in the past, and he has always been very reliable. He comes highly recommended," I continued, "and you don't get such a reputation for nothing. And besides, he's Uncle Sam's brother-in-law."

"What about the setter?" my husband continued. "Could he have switched the diamond for a fake?"

"The jeweler said there was no way that could have happened."

"So, let's move on," he said logically. "What about the person who brought it from South Africa?" That was too far-fetched, we decided. He's Grandma's close friend. "What about Grandma's sister-in-law Aunt Pearl, who gave her the earrings originally?" That was equally unrealistic, we both agreed. We had known Aunt Pearl, and she would never have told Grandma they were real diamonds if they weren't. Someone switched the stone, we both said, but who?

"That leaves us with one more suspect," said my husband. "The one who sold the earrings to Aunt Pearl."

Was that a long shot, or reasonable? As we talked on and on, we faintly remembered Grandma telling us that she had a reliable connection with this original seller.

We went over the list of suspects again. While in actuality it could have been any one of them, we had no substantial evidence one way or the other. But we were still left with a fake diamond.

"Listen," my husband continued. "Grandma thinks this diamond is real. If we call her to tell her it isn't, it will cause her tremendous aggravation. On the other hand, we can't just ignore this and not tell her, because she expects us to give this ring to her new granddaughter and we can't give her a fake diamond."

"Maybe," I suggested, "we should buy a real diamond and

present it to Simon's bride from Grandma and save Grandma the aggravation?"

We talked about this option, but decided against it. We did not like the idea of fooling anyone, and besides, Grandma had the second earring. It is conceivable that on one of her future visits, she would compare the two stones, and the switch might be discovered.

What should we do? We decided to sleep on it.

The next morning we rehashed the whole situation and went over all the possibilities again. It seemed to us more likely that the switch took place somewhere between the time Grandma received this gift and the time that it was sent to us than to think it happened once it reached us. And we thought of a way to prove it. Grandma could have her second earring checked. If it was a fake, then at least we would know on which side of the ocean the swindle occurred. If, in fact, the original seller had cheated her, then she should know to claim a loss. We decided to make the call.

Her reaction caught us off guard.

"Fake! What do you mean a fake?" Grandma's voice quivered. "My diamond is definitely not a fake. I have an appraisal certificate and insurance. It was appraised as a real diamond. Where's my diamond, children?" She was understandably distraught. "Diamonds should never be let out of one's sight!" That hurt, but I knew I deserved it.

"Mom," my husband said, "maybe your diamond earrings

were switched sometime since the appraisal. Maybe you should check it again."

"Maybe *I* should check it again? Maybe *you* should check it again!"

From across the ocean we tried to explain that the people we were dealing with were honest.

"Well," she said, "you may *think* they're honest. But I want that stone checked by a diamond expert. I know a good one, and I'll give you his address. I want you to show it to him. If he confirms it's a fake…"

"Then we're in big trouble," my husband interjected.

"You bet," said Grandma. "If yours is a fake, we're going to the police," she added solemnly.

You can well imagine how nervous I was on the way to Grandma's diamond expert. Especially because I knew I had been negligent for letting the diamond out of my sight. I handed the ring to the diamond expert and explained that there was a question about the ring's authenticity.

He examined it for a while with his loupe, rubbed it with sandpaper, and proclaimed, "This stone is a real diamond, no doubt about it."

I was so ecstatic I could hardly pay attention to the diamond dealer as he continued talking. But I forced myself to concentrate on his words as the pieces of the puzzle finally fell into place. I flew home to tell my husband and call Grandma.

Late that night before I fell asleep, I thought about the innocent misunderstandings and mistakes that occur in our daily lives that throw us into panic and lead us to accuse, and sometimes even malign, people who intend no harm. Feeling a lot calmer, I had a chance to review the words of the diamond expert. "How could the jeweler and the setter have made such a mistake?" I had asked the diamond dealer as he handed me back the ring.

"This whole thing is not surprising to me," he had answered. "Not surprising at all." He explained that a jeweler who deals mainly with gold is not always an expert in diamonds, and the setter might not have been an expert either. "They could be fooled into thinking that such flawlessness can only be found in a fake stone," he maintained. "Only an expert can discern conclusively."

❧

Although there may be a difference of opinion as to who is primarily at fault in this episode, there should be no disagreement on one point: When a loss is involved, there is a common human tendency to search for "the culprit," and to pin the blame on someone, regardless of the strength of the evidence.

Ethics of the Fathers (1:1) teaches us, "Be deliberate in judgment." If we are willing to "take it slow," and "go over the facts again," we are more likely to avoid instant judgments, which lead to slurs and denunciations that can prove to be embarrassing and that, so very often, we come to sorely regret.

26.

Leaving Us High & Dry

Spring was fast turning to summer. From past experience I knew that if I didn't do something soon, my spirited second-grader would be climbing the walls and giving me the run-around during the interminable summer vacation.

Just stop procrastinating, said an inner voice, *and get down to business if you want this thing to get off the ground.*

I had the idea of getting five mothers together to form a merry-go-round camp, similar to the well-known playgroup idea. The camp would function five days a week. Each day one mother would take all five children and have the other days off.

Eva and I were the first two members in this alliance.

Naomi got my message on her voice mail and left her reply on my answering machine. She would be thrilled to join in.

I bumped into Anne coming out of the bank. It didn't take too much convincing for her to become number four.

Just one more mother of a second-grader would tie this up. It dawned on me that Debra Fox had mentioned that she was buying some play equipment for her backyard. I reached her later that day and when she agreed, the membership in this great collaboration was closed.

Our first week was a huge success. The mothers felt it was a cohesive group, and the kids looked happy. Everything seemed to click. Then I got a call from Naomi Engel.

"I heard a rumor —" As soon as I heard that introduction, I had an intuitive feeling that there was trouble brewing.

Oh no, I moaned inwardly. Why spoil a perfectly calm Tuesday morning? I had such a sense of dread that I actually interrupted her to ask if she was sure she wanted to tell me. Naomi said she was positive I would want to know that Debra had pulled out.

"She pulled out of what?" I asked, not following.

"Debra's daughter is going to another camp." Naomi answered, obviously not in the mood for guessing games. "Would you believe that Debra would do that? Just take Mimi out without letting us know? You go into these things with decent people — or at least you think they are, and look what they do!" My friend Naomi was probably unaware that at this point she was practically yelling into the phone.

"Maybe there's been some mistake —" I ventured, but I was cut short.

"Listen, I don't spread rumors with no basis. I got this from a very reliable source."

I wasn't sure in which direction to take the conversation, so for a moment I hesitated.

"You don't believe me?" she asked in an offended tone. "Hold on a minute; I'll even check this out again."

Before I could respond, I was left holding the line, while Naomi was apparently verifying the facts on her other phone.

She came back a few minutes later and continued where she had left off. "I know it defies the imagination. Debra did put Mimi in another group. I asked again, and it's true. Where is her sense of responsibility?" Naomi was yelling again. "How could someone ignore a commitment and leave us stranded in the middle of everything?"

I was listening, but I did not have much to add. It certainly didn't sound good.

"Wednesday is her rotation day." Naomi reminded me. "What does she think we're going to do tomorrow?"

"Did you speak to her directly?" I inquired. "Did you ask her why she pulled out?"

"No, I didn't. I'm just too upset to call. I know it won't come out nice."

I paused a moment and considered whether I wanted to jump into the frying pan. "Maybe I'll call," I said finally. "We all have to know what we're in for tomorrow."

Debra picked up after the first ring. We chatted for a few moments. I was listening for some wiliness, duplicity, or guile in her voice, but she sounded like the same amiable Debra.

Finally I came out with it. "I heard you are sending Mimi to another group."

"Yes," she answered immediately.

So it really is true, I thought with disbelief.

"I wanted to stick it out, but Mimi just wasn't happy. I tried another group with children a little younger, and she fits in better."

I was just about to ask her why she did not let us know — what did she think we would do now? — when I heard her continue.

"I was planning to tell all of you tomorrow when you came. But nuncha worry," Debra teased in her winning way, "I'm still keeping my day."

There are times when we have to discuss a person's improper behavior in order to deal with the matter. This discussion is valid as long as we keep in mind that the second witness in the drama was not yet called to the stand. If we directly approach that person we might find out that it's just not the way it seems.

27.

Waiting on Pins and Needles

"**W**hose is that?" I thought out loud as I tried to stuff my coat into my brother's already overcrowded front closet. I was referring to a striking green jacket, with a black velvet collar, dwarfed between two overcoats. Evidently, it was a recent acquisition, judging from the price tag still peeking out from the sleeve. When I complimented my sister-in-law on her elegant new purchase, she told me that after buying it she realized that it didn't fit her properly, and I would be doing her a big favor if I took it. I saw right away that it would be too large for me, but it was so lovely that I felt it would be worthwhile investing in an alteration.

My cousin Helen, who owns a dress shop, had recently given me the number of a dressmaker named Samantha Brown. A long-time patron of Mrs. Brown, Helen could attest to her skill and professionalism. The only drawback was location, since the dressmaker lived in an area of Johannesburg which was quite unsafe.

I contacted Mrs. Brown. Daytime hours being safer than evening, we arranged an appointment for the following afternoon at 2:15.

I arrived on time. Standing outside a tall green gate amidst plush green shrubbery, I rang the bell. A young girl who introduced herself as Samantha's daughter came to the gate. Having heard why I had come, she explained that her mother was not at home, but if I would take a seat and wait, she should arrive shortly. I followed her as she led me into a tastefully decorated kitchenette and I sat down with her at the table, where she was busy sorting out photographs. 2:15 became 2:30, which then became 2:45. I could see that Miss Brown was uncomfortable. As the minutes ticked away, she became more and more apologetic. From time to time, she glanced at the wall clock, where the minute hand was continuing its ascent.

A chime signaled 3:00, and our eyes met. Evidently sensing that something needed to be said, she cleared her throat. Then, forcing a smile, she said contritely, "I really am so sorry about my mother. It's not that she's unreliable — she's just somewhat forgetful."

A little before 3:15, Samantha walked in. Seeing me sitting there, her hand flew to her mouth, partially stifling a cry of, "Oh, no!" She proceeded to apologize profusely for having forgotten our appointment. Throughout the fitting, she kept reiterating how sorry she was. I was moved by her sincerity and so I assured her that I understood that such things happen.

The following week Samantha phoned to arrange a convenient time for a second fitting. She said she was going out but would be home by 6:00, so we arranged to meet at her home at 6:15. I asked my husband to accompany me since, as I mentioned, she lived in an unsafe area, and it would be dark by then.

We arrived promptly, stood outside the tall green gate, and rang the bell. A domestic servant came to the gate and informed us that her employer was not at home. I explained that I had an appointment with her employer, who would no doubt be arriving any minute. She led us through the garden, into the house, and seated us in the lounge. A few minutes later she left the house to go to her quarters in the backyard, locking the security gate outside the back door behind her.

We settled down and waited. Occasionally, we checked our watches. Before long they synchronized at 6:30. Some small talk passed between us. Mostly we sat solemnly. By 6:45 I was becoming irritated. I telephoned my cousin to inquire whether she had a mobile phone number for Samantha. Helen said that she did not, but she added that the previous week, she had bumped into the dressmaker, who told her how distressed she was that she had forgotten our appointment.

"During our conversation," Helen said, "she repeated several times how sorry she felt about being so late."

"I see how bad she felt," I snapped back at my cousin. "She's done it again."

We continued waiting. I was becoming increasingly perturbed. As I impatiently paced the floor, working up my temper, my husband pointed out that there are at least a hundred sound reasons why a person could be unavoidably delayed.

"True," I admitted, "but in this case there's only *one* explanation for the dressmaker's tardiness — the same reason as last time — irresponsibility, unreliability, and disorganization. She probably doesn't own an appointment book and even if she did, she would most probably forget to look at it!"

By 7:00, my husband and I decided that there was no point waiting around any longer. I wrote a curt note and we got up to leave. Or at least we thought so. As we opened the front door, we realized that the front security gate was locked. Now what? We conferred for a minute and decided that the most logical step would be to try to locate the domestic servant whose room was somewhere outside behind the house. We called out once. No reply. Then a little louder. We opened the window and called again, but no one appeared. My husband said that we should go to another part of the house and call her from a window which faced a different part of the yard. I suggested that we go into the kitchen and call from that window, as most domestic servants' rooms are situated behind the kitchen.

We entered the kitchen, and I stopped short, ingesting what I saw. Turning to my husband, I sputtered, "You're not going to believe this, but I think we're in the wrong house. This was not the kitchen I sat in with her daughter last week!"

Immediately, I took out my mobile phone and dialed Samantha's number.

"Where are you?" Samantha questioned anxiously, as soon as I identified myself. "I was so worried about you when you didn't come. You know this is not a safe street."

We were eventually let out of the house and went next door to the dressmaker's home, which had the same green shrubbery and the very same green gate.

Have you ever left someone waiting while you never showed up?

Was your mistake:

Right time, wrong place! (You got the address wrong.)

Right place, wrong time! (You thought it was next Monday.)

Wrong time, wrong place — and you wondered where everyone is.

Right time, right place — or at least you thought so. Then someone noticed your watch. It was still on daylight savings time.

Or conversely, were you ever stood up? Please consider one of the above.

28.

A Lot of Hot Water

It was Friday afternoon, and the water was hot. It was Michal's turn for the shower.

"Michal," said my wife to our nine-year-old daughter, "please go easy on the hot water. Your father and I still need to take showers."

The warning was in vain. Lukewarm describes my shower only charitably; my wife's shower was certainly worse.

From the lips outward, my wife and I tried to actualize the great principle of "judging favorably." "Maybe I used too much water for the dishes," said my wife.

"Or maybe there's some other explanation," I offered.

In our hearts, however, we agreed on one thing: our budding adolescent was guilty of yet another act of gross self-centeredness.

That night the real culprit revealed himself, as a trickle of water appeared from the crack in the wall where the bathtub meets the tiles. (Aha! So that's why that mysterious crack had been developing for the last couple of months!) In the morning, that trickle became a whoosh of spurting water.

Monday morning, the plumber replaced the rusty pipe, which had been rotting away in our wall for who knows how long. It had sprung a leak and was apparently to blame for countless many instances of "inconsiderate behavior."

❧

Too bad it's not that easy to replace our rusty "heart pipes" so that we can learn to judge others — yes, even our children — favorably.

29.

Crying Over Spilled Milk

At first, it hardly bothered her. It was a dull pain she hoped would just go away. Weeks — no, months — passed before it was severe enough to compel her to make that call to the doctor's office.

She remembers that day, undoubtedly the coldest day of the winter. She filled out forms and was sent for tests.

Some time later the results came back.

Had it been a year already? A year of all-too-familiar hospital corridors, harried nurses, cold, steel machines. And a lot of rest. So much of the time, she needed to rest.

How lucky I am to have Tami and Lynn. What would I do without those angels? This thought passed through Lillie's mind countless times, and each time, she offered a prayer of thanks for that blessing to the One Above.

Truth be told, what *would* Lillie have done without her two oldest daughters? Here and there she managed to do what she could, but the lion's share fell on their teenage shoulders, which seemed to be broadening by the day. Balancing school and household chores, they pulled her through, and their home was able to continue functioning.

"Functioning" is not really an accurate description, because the girls helped run the house in all its aspects. Besides doing the laundry, ironing shirts, mending, and shopping, they faithfully prepared the daily meals for the whole family. How many mothers could boast such capable, reliable daughters?

Lillie prayed for strength and patience, and for acceptance. She prayed that she would never lose her joy for living or her appreciation of the manifold blessings that surrounded her. And she prayed for the day when she would not have to depend so much on Tami and Lynn.

It was Wednesday again. That meant another appointment. The younger children wouldn't be home until late in the afternoon. Tami and Lynn would be at friends all morning studying for exams.

Today they won't have to help. It's not fair to them. They are always there when I need them, and now they will surely need extra time to study. When I come home, I'll push myself and do what I can on my own.

Tami came home first. She read the note signed "Love, Mom" that urged her to eat lunch and continue with her studies.

By the time Lynn walked in, the smells of onion soup and grilled cheese that Tami had prepared permeated the house. Five hours of steady studying had made her more than ready to eat. The sisters sat sipping hot soup, reviewing their morning, and sympathizing with each other about the number of pages they still had to brood over. As usual they discussed the division of labor for that day. "Divide and conquer," Lynn would say. Of course they would also study — later.

As she was clearing the table, ever-exuberant Lynn was hit with an inspiration. Pulling at her sister's sleeve, she bubbled, "Tami, picture Mom coming home and sitting down to homemade apple pie. Can't you see her throwing her arms around us, telling us we're like angels sent from Heaven?"

The kitchen echoed with the whir of the mixer, Lynn's boisterous singing, and Tami's quiet humming to the accompaniment of their favorite tape.

Lillie came home mid-afternoon. The girls recognized the sound of their mother's car before they heard her footsteps and then her, "Hello, who's home? Where are my angels?"

In no time, they sensed it. They heard it in her voice and saw it in her movements. Today's treatment had taken its toll on their mother. Tami took her hand and led her to the kitchen. Lynn pulled out a chair, while Tami presented the apple pie. Lillie sat wordlessly as her daughter cut a slice and set it before her with a freshly brewed cup of coffee.

"How did it go today, Mom?" Lynn asked first, slipping

into a chair beside her mother.

"How was your test, Lynnie?" Lillie interjected, thinking of a way to divert the conversation. "And yours, Tami?" she turned to her elder daughter. By the time she had heard them out and shared their stories, her coffee was cold.

"Here, Mom, I'll bring you a fresh hot cup," Tami jumped up.

"Only if you promise that you'll run right up, both of you, and study for tomorrow's exam."

"OK, one coffee for you and back to the salt mines for us."

The hot coffee was in front of her. Before she had a chance to thank her "angels," they had already reached the top of the stairs.

Sitting alone in the silent kitchen, studying the fluted edges of the piecrust, Lillie felt her eyes stinging. In an instant, tears were spilling down her cheeks. Burying her face in trembling hands, she surrendered to those tears that poured forth unchecked. What was it that triggered those tears? Maybe it was exhaustion, or perhaps her pain. Or could it have been the apple pie?

Whatever it was, once the tears started, they refused to stop.

Lillie, Lillie, stop. Enough. The girls will worry if they hear you. If they come in, your tears will frighten them. Drink your coffee before the second cup gets cold.

She reached for the milk. It was almost empty.

Forcing herself up from the chair, she moved slowly towards the refrigerator and reached for a carton of milk. Her hand shook involuntarily as she began to pour. She was weak, her eyes still clouded by tears. As she was pouring the milk, the carton slipped from her hand, leaving Lillie with a mess of milk on the table and chair, and a large puddle on the floor.

How could she muster up the strength to pick up that carton, let alone clean up the spill?

Lillie, just do it, she commanded herself. She made her way to the garage and came back with a mop and two cloths.

As she was wiping the table, the doorbell rang. Lynn bounded down the stairs.

"How are you, Lynnie?"

"Uncle Abe, how nice to see you. Mom's in the kitchen drinking coffee. Go right in. I'll take your coat."

"It's good seeing you, Lynnie. I usually come to see Mom in the mornings. It's lucky for me that the afternoon worked out better today, so I have a chance to see one of my favorite nieces."

Lynn flashed him her winning smile before charging up the stairs.

"Lillie, I'm here," Abe called out as he headed for the kitchen.

Lillie turned as he came to the doorway. When she saw his dropped jaw, his raised eyebrows, and the deeply disturbed look on his face, she realized what he was seeing.

Here I am, his sister, a sick woman, a face streaked with tears, looking like I'm on the verge of collapse, mopping the floor!"

Her brother was beside himself. "Where are those girls!" he bellowed. "What in the world are they doing?"

"They're upstairs studying, Abe. I know what you're thinking, but — "

"Upstairs? While you slave away?"

"Abe, you don't understand, I sent them up bec– "

"And they went? Instead of helping you?" he roared, bolting out of the room in mid-sentence. He headed for the stairs, taking them two at a time. She had no strength to chase after him.

Lillie could hear him bawling them out all the way from the kitchen. She knew her girls would politely hold their tongues.

When he finally came down, somewhat calmed, Lillie was at the table, picking at some crumbs. She invited her devoted, well-meaning brother to join her.

"Listen, Lillie, even if you're not well, you must take the time to teach the girls consideration, give them more responsibilities. What's the point of all their learning if they haven't been taught those things?"

Lillie tried to stop him.

"No, let me finish."

She did, although she knew he would be sorry later, when he would finally give her a chance to speak.

❧

"That Lynn Peterson should be ashamed of herself. You should have seen the way she treats her mother. And I was there when it happened."

In the book of Exodus (23:1), we learn "Be careful about believing rumors." This includes information about people and descriptions of events, even when these are eyewitness reports. Maybe the speaker exaggerates. Maybe he spoke out of jealousy or spite. We should not accept the report at face value, because we did not witness the facts.

But even when we were there, when we ourselves did bear witness to undesirable behavior, we should be wary of passing judgment, as this story once again illustrates: seeing should not be a license to believe.

30

Watch Out

The glass showcase rotated ever so slowly, first taking it away, out of her sight, and then teasingly bringing it closer once more. It allowed her just a few seconds to inspect and admire, and then it was whisked off again.

The patent leather band was deep fuchsia, its face a shade of party pink. Its numbers were big, black, and easy to read. Ilana hoped it would be hers one day.

Her friend Dina had a watch, a green one. She could *almost* tell time. Simi's watch was white. But Ilana thought that nothing could be nicer than the one in the case. And she counted the days.

"For your birthday, Ilana," her mother had promised. "You know it's only two months from now, dear. Then you'll be six. I'll teach you how to tell time, and then you can…"

Mother and daughter sat together on the couch and day-dreamed together about the myriad things a six-year-old can do with the help of a watch. Ilana could stay in the backyard until dinnertime without her mother having to call her in. She would know how long she would have to wait until the cupcakes could come out of the oven. And she could check her watch to see when her father was expected home, so she could set out his slippers.

"How much more, Mommy? Huh? How many more days to go?" Mrs. Landers brought her five-year-old daughter to the calendar, so they could count the squares and mark them off. Ilana was satisfied as she turned two pages and saw the big, red circle around Wednesday, the day she would finally be six.

The days passed, the weeks went by, and at long last two pages of the calendar had been marked off.

It lay there on the night table, right beside her bed that Wednesday morning, wrapped in flowered paper with dangling pink and yellow ribbons. Even though Ilana knew exactly what the small box contained, her excitement was not one bit less.

She skipped up the school steps and raced to her classroom. She would catch Mrs. Hammer the first thing, before she went into the room. Ilana knew that her teacher would share her excitement over the present. Six is really big, and here was the watch to prove it.

The world has changed. You can see it all over, and I, a veteran first-grade teacher for more than three decades now, can tell you that the difference is blatant in the classroom.

A perfect example is what happened to me last week.

After that big rain on Tuesday night, I walked cautiously down the stairs to the basement. Halfway down, I knew I had a problem. The toys from my grandchildren's last visit were floating quietly in the water. My laundry basket full of neatly folded towels was half immersed. Two cardboard boxes of clothing ready to be stored away were saturated.

I live in an area near the ocean, with a very high water table. When it rains heavily, the water soaks the ground to the point where the earth can't absorb more water. As a result, the excess water seeps into my basement and causes flooding. This happens usually one or two times per year.

Of course the damage could have been much worse. Since I know my basement is at risk, I prepare for the eventuality of flooding by keeping the floor relatively uncluttered.

Wading in, I salvaged the non-waterproof toys, threw the towels back into the machine, and laid out the clothing to dry. I hadn't completely finished, but I'd done enough to prevent any further damage until I would return from school.

It's a good thing that I always leave leeway in my morning routine for the unexpected setbacks and emergencies every normal house has. I certainly needed every extra minute that day.

Hurriedly, I called the cleaning service, asking them to come in the afternoon with their large vacuum that sucks up water. After that, I called the school secretary to tell her I would be a little late.

Maneuvering carefully through traffic and taking some side streets, I pulled into the school's parking lot only a little later than usual.

I rushed up the front stairs, through the door, and down the hall towards my classroom.

There at the door stood one of my first-graders, with her arm stretched out. She was pointing to her watch, letting me know that I was late.

Could you believe the chutzpah? In my days, no child would dream of doing such a nervy thing.

I walked right by her; my practiced look let her know what I thought of her antics.

I would have made her stay outside. However, I did not want her to miss the lecture I was planning to give to the class on proper respect for a teacher.

Many a teacher has blown the whistle a little too soon. And many a student has suffered public embarrassment for an offense that was never confirmed or investigated. These pupils were never given a chance to explain, because their

accusers never considered that there might be an explanation pending.

Teachers, educators — watch out. Although you must keep your charges in line, you must be careful not to jump the gun.

And when a mistake is made, even a teacher should not discount making an apology.

31.

On Friendship

Friendship is not only sharing the good times. It means being there on rough days too.

Joel and I had been friends since we were kids. When Joel's father passed away suddenly last summer, I was out of town. Of course I called right away but never managed to reach him. I found out he was sitting *shivah* at his father's home. When I got back, I drove over straight from the airport.

As I walked in, so many familiar sights came into view. Together, Joel and I had visited this house often. There was the umbrella stand, the mirror (now covered), and pictures of the children and grandchildren proudly displayed on the walls of the foyer, including new additions since my last visit.

I turned the corner and saw Joel. His two brothers were sitting near him. Joel's uncle was also there. I took a seat on the side near my good buddy.

Joel was speaking with someone I did not recognize. He looked tired. Although it was just the first day, it was obvious he had already done a lot of talking. There was plenty to say about his father, and Joel had a special way of expressing things that he remembered. As I sat down he looked in my direction. Our eyes met.

He shook his head at me and said, "You're not allowed to be here."

I figured I didn't hear right. But, you understand, it's not the kind of thing you ask a person to repeat. Not then. So I just ignored it. *Look,* I thought, *it's a tough time for anyone, and especially hard because he and his father were so close. Leave him alone.*

I asked Joel about the details of the last few days. He filled me in on all that had happened.

I thought I could push it out of my mind, but I found that the comment kept coming back to me. When there was a lull in the conversation, it was right there confusing me.

Did I understand correctly? Was Joel sending me a message?

I started to tell him how I had tried to call but the line was constantly busy. He listened. Was he annoyed that I hadn't made more of an effort to reach him? *You're not allowed to be here because you should have made sure to be with me at the funeral or at least to call right away.* Is that what he meant? A few other versions went through my head, but they all fell flat.

I sat there, but half the time I was tuned out. *Since when is a shivah call selective? What kind of business is this? You can come. You can't. This is crazy. I'm a good close friend!*

Joel turned to acknowledge someone who just walked in. *"You're not allowed to be here"* kept replaying itself in my mind. Should I leave? That didn't seem right either. So I sat there doing the best I could to keep the conversation normal.

People came and went. It was getting late. Except for two people talking to Joel's brother, the room had emptied.

Then Joel turned to me. He smiled his familiar smile.

"I could see by your face that you didn't get what I was saying."

You bet I didn't, I thought, but did not answer, waiting for him to continue.

"I guess this isn't the time to be funny. And I wasn't trying to be. I was sure you would understand me right away. You shouldn't be here at a time like this, my good friend — because I'm too happy when I see you".

He's a devoted friend. From past experience, you know him to be reasonable and considerate. Now his behavior is disconcerting, if not downright maddening.

Logic says — it's not likely that he has lost his senses. More likely, it is we who have not yet found the solution to this perplexity.

In fact, for a sensible person like this, the more unreasonable his behavior appears, the easier it should be to realize that there must be something else brewing here.

32.

Gimme a Break!

When the heating system broke down, I just hoped I wasn't next.

It had been a long, challenging winter. First, my mother was bedridden as the result of a fall. After endless attempts, we still could not find her the proper help, so I went daily to give her a hand. Right afterwards, our son was "asked to leave" school. The effort it took to "reinstate" him took its toll on all of us. Just around that time, my husband Sammy and his partner split up, so Sammy started his own business. For months, nights were like days in our house, as he struggled to set his feet on solid ground. I was there throughout, supporting and encouraging him. To top it all off, our heating system broke down, and two experts could not locate the problem.

Until that point I was a bit winded, a bit strained, a bit cold, but gliding. Then I came down with the flu, and that knocked me out completely. Two of my children also caught it, but I guess they have more resilience, because they were up and about after three days. I just could not get back to myself.

Now don't get me wrong. I know that on a broad scope my problems are really neither exceptional nor insurmountable. I keep telling myself how thankful I have to be for hardships that are bearable and how lucky I am in so many different ways. I know, and I try to keep remembering. Nonetheless, I was exhausted.

My dear friend Becky, who held my hand during those trying, frosty months, decided that I needed some pampering, so she invited Sammy and me for a long weekend, insisting that all I would have to do was appear at meals. I am usually not one to be coddled, but Becky impressed on me how even a mini-vacation would do me a world of good, so I let myself be convinced that this was the time to allow myself a little spoiling.

We had no problem farming out the children. Sammy made plans to have the office covered while I was preparing to close up the house and reveling in the thought of being taken care of.

One afternoon, three days before our planned departure, my children were playing upstairs with our neighbors, the Gellers. When they came down, they reminded me that the Gellers were inviting family and a few close friends and neighbors for the weekend to celebrate their 20th anniversary. It had completely slipped my mind.

That threw a damper on our plans. Accepting Becky's invitation meant missing Carmella's. That was not such a simple choice, especially since Carmella Geller not only comes whenever we are hosting an event, but pitches in with both good cheer and elbow grease. I had been so out of sorts lately that I hadn't offered to help, and now I would not even be able to be there.

"If I am not for myself, who will be for me," I defended myself, trying to squelch my pangs of conscience. I was planning to go upstairs to apologize for my absence, but before I could, Carmella was at my door. She had heard the children say that I was going away. What basically followed was that she was happy I would get some well-deserved rest, sorry I wouldn't be there, and in lieu of our presence, could they have the use of our apartment? That morning they'd gotten a call canceling on an apartment, which left her without a place for her in-laws, who needed to stay at a ground level apartment, preferably near her. Our place would be ideal, and she would be ever so grateful.

How could I refuse? How could I tell her that I had no strength to get the apartment ready for guests? But strength was something I definitely did not have, so I felt I had to tell her about my hesitation.

"Heaven forbid! I don't want you to touch a thing," Carmella protested. "You of all people don't have to worry about that anyway! Your apartment always sparkles."

"But you know how it is when you're having guests," I half pleaded. But to no avail.

"Don't be silly," Carmella chided. "Don't even think of doing anything. It's more than fine the way it is. And you don't have to worry about anyone leaving a mess," my neighbor assured me. "They're just two people and won't disturb a thing. You'll get the apartment back just as you left it."

So what could I say? Carmella had it all worked out.

Becky, however, did not buy the argument. "I know you," she warned me. "You'll be busy turning your house into a five-star hotel. Then you'll lose out on the whole point of your vacation." I assured her that I would try not to overdo it, but we both knew the truth.

Since it was only Tuesday, I figured it gave me enough time to pace myself. If I could plan a sensible strategy, I could work slowly, doing the minimum each day and still leave the apartment in decent condition.

Becky was right. Changing the linens, rearranging the closet to provide hanging space, that was nothing. It was the scrubbing and polishing that kept me up till late at night. What could I do? That's just the way I am.

By the time I finished packing a bag for each child, and then a suitcase for us, I was too exhausted to recall exactly which child had revealed our plans to the Gellers in the first place. "This is all their fault," I muttered resentfully, as I zipped the suitcase closed.

Stop that this minute, I chastised the image in the mirror. *If you didn't want to do the favor, you should have said no. What's the point of agreeing and then faulting every-one else because of your standards of clean?* And with that, I wiped a smudge from the mirror.

Friday morning we got up early, ate breakfast on the run, threw the last items into the bags, and rushed out so the children wouldn't be late for school. At long last we could start our vacation.

Was it worth it? I suppose it was. All in all, I did have a wonderful time. Becky was a hostess par excellence. It was only those nagging thoughts that kept getting in the way.

Why can other people open their homes so easily, and for me it's such a problem?

Don't be so hard on yourself, you're under the weather.

Maybe they will invite the grandchildren in, and they'll turn the house upside down!

Vacillating between feelings of remorse and anxiety about the condition in which I would find my apartment, I just could not relax.

Even so, I arrived home on Monday in a much better state than I had left. Sammy turned the key in the door and pushed it open. The first thing that hit me were the lights. They had been left on. That set the mood. I felt the tension starting in my hands, slowly crawling up my arms. I had not yet looked around, but I braced myself for the worst.

Suspiciously, I made my way through the rooms. Before I even walked into the kitchen I could hear the water. One of the faucets had been left dripping!

How careless, I thought with annoyance. Whenever I see things like that, my automatic reaction is, "Where was the mother?" Certain things a person should take with them from their home. Didn't anyone ever teach these people common courtesy? Like screwing a cap back on the bottle when you finish, shutting off lights when you leave the room, putting the cover back on the toothpaste, closing drawers and cabinets when you finish with them, and making sure the faucet doesn't drip!

Who knows what else awaited me!

I peeked into the bedroom and saw, not surprisingly, that the linen had been left on the bed. Couldn't they have stripped the beds? Did they think we would use the same linens?

I still have not mentioned what bothered me the most. I searched the whole house, I even opened drawers, but it was not there. To me it was inconceivable that they did not even have the courtesy to leave a note. Wouldn't you think they would at least have said something? OK, I'm not the type to expect a gift, but not even a few words? All I can say is, "It takes all kinds."

Come on, be nice! my inner voice piped up again. *Maybe they couldn't find a pen and paper,* I tried generously, and then went to put the sheets in the washing machine.

Carmella! The thought hit me abruptly. I must go up and

wish her a mazel tov. (Talk about common courtesy.)

A small breeze met me as I stepped out of the house. It must have cooled me off somewhat, and I realized how tense I had become from that "arraignment."

OK. Let the prosecution rest. More for your sake than anyone else's, I advised myself as I climbed the stairs to the Gellers.

Carmella answered the door. As we sat down, I could see she looked tired, and the house was in a bit of disarray, but her quiet afterglow told me that all had gone well.

"So tell me all about your anniversary weekend," I urged, sitting down next to her on the sofa.

"I meant to come to see how you are feeling and thank you for your offer," she replied.

Offer? But there was no time to ask questions. She was going on, and I was doing my best to listen.

"I have been so busy trying to put my house back together, freezing all the leftovers, returning tables, chairs, and all the cake platters people left. But I was planning to come to thank you for your offer."

Why does she keep saying my "offer?" I wondered once more.

Carmella leaned back into the couch cushions, making desperate attempts to stifle a persistent yawn. "The weekend was a smashing success, but I am bushed. You know how it goes with these things. You plan and plan, but unexpected changes always come up. Friday morning the tables showed up, each of them smaller than what we had ordered. We panicked. You can't make people sit on the floor! Then later that morning my father-in-law called us saying that he was not feeling well. We could not imagine making a celebration without our parents, but my mother-in-law insisted that Dad simply was not up to it. We kept calling all Friday afternoon to see if there was any improvement, but it seems his fever was still high, and in the end, would you believe it?"

"Believe what?" I asked, trying to keep up with her story.

"Would you believe they never came?"

We are constantly involved in drawing conclusions, based on assumptions. But are we careful to ascertain whether those assumptions are valid? Based on our carelessly formulated conclusions, we righteously look askance at the ignobility and inferiority that surround us.

Why are we so quick to condemn? What do we get out of it? Downgrading others is a way of enhancing our own importance. Like a ride on a seesaw, we feel we are automatically raised when we push others down. "I would never do that!" is what we are telling the world.

Arrogantly condemning others is wrong, even when based on truth. How much more so when based on error.

33.

On the Face of It

"Good morning, Mr. Robinson," a student said, whipping past me as I was getting out of my car.

"Same to you," I called back. "And have a good day, Brad," I added. *How could a day like this be anything but good,* I thought to myself, as I flicked a new purple bud that must have sprung up overnight. Whistling my way into the school building, I sensed the high spirits that permeated the air. After a cold and snowy winter, it looked like spring was here at last.

I paused for a second at the door of my classroom, scanning the scene, scenting the mood of the morning. Even before I bellowed out my animated greeting, only to be met with a unanimous "killjoy" expression, I knew I'd have to give it my all to hold the interest of this restless crew. On cue, the boys reluctantly shuffled back to their seats. Books and pens made their appearance. But I could see that although they were sitting here in the classroom, their minds were still outside. A few of them even had one foot in the aisle, ready to stampede out at the earliest possible second. When the bell finally rang, it took less than a minute for the last boy to race through the door.

By the time I followed them out to the yard, they were already well into their games. My day for yard patrol, I wove my way between players to a bench at the side of the schoolyard, amidst yelps and shouts that seemed to be announcing, "We love spring!"

A ball rolled by. I grabbed it and threw it back. Breathing in a big gulp of springtime, I settled back to survey my surroundings. In the far corner of the yard was a familiar tree, which had bent and broken under the weight of the winter snow. To the left, two squirrels were chasing each other, one of them with an acorn in its mouth. Overhead, the chitter-chatter of the birds made me wonder how they had made their way back north so fast.

My vision then focused upon a parade of ants making a grand detour to avoid my shoe. I was fascinated by this busy procession, carrying bits of food almost as big as they were. Do they ever get tired or stop to rest?

Loud noises interrupted my thoughts. I looked up. At the other end of the yard, two boys were arguing. I could not make out exactly what they were saying, but angry shouts and flailing arms were unmistakable. As they continued, more boys gathered around them. At first I thought I would give them a chance to settle it themselves. *Look how nicely the ants get along,* I thought to myself with a chuckle. *All working together so peacefully*, I marveled as I watched them marching by.

The argument didn't stop, and as their voices escalated, I decided it was time to intervene.

I approached the circle and joined the growing crowd. Donny and Andy were in the middle. Faces red and all charged up, they were both airing their grievances.

"Why do you keep saying I started? You know you started this fight," Donny accused.

"Me? I did not. It was your fault in the first place," Andy yelled, defensively.

"You're a liar!" Donny roared, raising his fist menacingly.

They both sounded angry and hurt, and it was only getting worse. From the looks of it, in another minute they would be at each other's necks.

"Hold it, fellas!" I interrupted the crossfire. "What's going on?"

They both looked at me and answered in unison, "He started it," each one pointing to the other.

This was by no means the first match I had refereed. All in all, I had a good record for forestalling all-out war.

"From my perspective up here..." I began, with an encouraging pinch to two flushed cheeks, "it seems to me that you are going around in circles, getting nowhere fast. Let's go back to the beginning," I suggested, "and try to sort this thing out."

Still breathing heavily, they stood tensely, but held their peace for the moment.

"Well?" I urged.

Empty expressions stared back at me.

Then I saw Andy's face brighten, as if he had hit on something.

"I know," he announced, throwing up his arms triumphantly, his voice insinuating that some revelation would be forthcoming. "Now I remember how we got into this fight, and I can prove that Donny started it," Andy declared with confidence, plainly pleased to see justice finally prevail. "Don't you remember how *you* started this? It was you who made a face at me. That's how it started, remember?"

Satisfied that he had won his case, Andy proceeded to imitate the face Donny had made. I looked at Donny to catch his reaction to this accusation, but he just stood there, watching Andy's features wrinkle up.

Arms hanging limply by his sides, eyes riveted to Andy's face, Donny watched him like a hawk, in silence. I wondered what there was about that expression that held his attention. I had a hunch the answer would surface in due course.

Sure enough, in another moment, the corners of Donny's mouth turned up. I knew that the mystery had been solved when an expression of clarity replaced his previously troubled visage.

He took a step towards Andy and put a hand on his friend's shoulder. With a big, toothy grin he pronounced, "Andy, I just didn't have my glasses on. I was not making a face. I was squinting!"

❧

It could be shoes that pinch, an upset stomach, sciatica, or a migraine headache. Yet, we could easily take that frown personally, assuming it is directed at us.

Misread facial expressions, misinterpreted body movements, can set off a chain reaction. One day your neighbor passes by, concentrating on something else. So he ignores you. Hmmmph. Next time he won't get any recognition from me.

And there you have it.

Unless proven otherwise, assume it's not you.

34.

Talking it Over

"**W**hen do we get to use all those things that we saved for a rainy day?"

The question was tossed to me by my seven-year-old, as I was racing against time to beat the morning deadline.

Early morning is not, in my opinion, the time for philosophical discussions. Besides, I was not exactly sure how to tackle that one, so I just shot him back one of my "not now" looks and told him that the more important question to deal with at that moment was "Where are your boots?" And, "Did you know that the van will be here in ten minutes and your breakfast is still untouched?"

At least I knew where his question was coming from. It was raining cats and dogs. No doubt he pictured us imminently cashing in on all those treasures he heard we were saving for that proverbial rainy day.

Through some minor miracle we found the boots — one right, one left, no less.

"Grab your umbrella and get going," I called out to Benjy.

Opening the door, I took one look and made an immediate turnabout. Was it within reason to let a child stand outside in this downpour? It made much more sense to call Linda, who had recently moved into the neighborhood and was the bus stop before me and ask her to give me a ring when her son, Joey, was picked up. What's the point of standing there in the pouring rain and getting to school wet and shivering?

After three rings I heard her hello.

"Hi. Good morning. It's Natalie. Sorry to bother you, but you probably noticed it's coming down in buckets. If you don't mind, could you call me when Joey gets picked up, so I won't have to send Benjy outside any earlier than necessary?"

The same voice responded curtly, "No, I can't."

I was still holding the receiver waiting for some explanation or apology, but all I heard was a click and then the tone that told me that Linda had hung up.

Bundling Benjy up the best I could, I sent him out to wait with whatever protection the umbrella offered.

No one has to explain to me what a hectic morning means. I've had plenty of my own. I know what it feels like to have ten things first in the pecking order. But my request was not outlandish. I had simply asked her to call me after Joey left, after all the emergencies had passed. Let us even assume that she hung up so quickly because something urgent still needed tending to. But there's a certain bottom line that normal, decent people do not cross. I would never answer a person so abruptly, no matter how much pressure I was under. And I certainly would not slam down the phone.

I threw myself into the morning chores, clearing the table, washing the dishes, all the while groping for a solution. Could she be angry with me? Impossible! Whatever for? She had only moved in recently. There hasn't even been enough time for a misunderstanding!

Her rudeness just boggled my mind! I kept thinking that the phone would ring at any moment and it would be Linda, with an explanation or an apology.

By noon it was rather obvious that it was not going to happen. Bottling this up was not helping me, so I reached for the phone and dialed my old faithful number that would surely help me get to the bottom of this.

My clever friend Anne has a flair for explaining things away. She can usually help me get my bearings and come to grips with any crisis.

When I reached the part about, "No, I can't," Anne laughed. I was not exactly expecting that reaction.

"Want to tell me what strikes you as funny?"

"I will," she answered, a trace of humor still in her voice. "But not this second. I have to run to get to my exercise class on time. I'll be back in about an hour and a half. Then have I got a story to tell you!"

I was not sure that a story was what I had called her for, but trusting Anne's knack for wit and wisdom, I waited anxiously for her call; all afternoon and into the evening.

What's going on? I thought. *I started off being annoyed about one call, now I'm annoyed about two! This is crazy.*

About 9:00 p.m., the phone rang. It was Anne. I listened intently, waiting. *This better be a good one,* I thought as I heard my friend's voice.

"First, let me tell you that story I promised you, and then I'll explain why I didn't call until now, OK?"

The order didn't matter, so I let her do it her way.

"Are you in the middle of something?" Anne asked politely.

"Yes. Listening to you."

"OK, wise guy, sit down and hear me out. Remember I told you about this lady who gives a mini-course on the art of garnishing?"

"Sort of," I affirmed, wondering where she was taking me.

"My friends who went last time loved it," Anne continued eagerly. "Each one came home with an arrangement of vegetable flowers, things like turnip lilies, beet asters, radish daisies, tomato roses, onion mums, cucumber leaves…"

Anne broke off, obviously waiting for some oohs and ahs.

"I'm listening, Anne, but you know this is not my thing," I begged off, at the same time hoping not to put a damper on her enthusiasm.

"Admit it, Natalie," Anne goaded, not a bit put off, "so much depends on presentation. Garnishing gives a dish that finished look," she gushed.

"I see you're really into this," I noted.

"You bet. Anyway, the course was scheduled for Tuesday at seven, and I did not want to miss it this time. So I made sure to finish supper early and sat everyone down to do homework. My husband always walks in promptly at seven, and he had already agreed that I should go. His supper sat covered on the table.

"It was ten to seven. I blew kisses to everyone, hoping I could trust them not to turn the house upside down in the ten minutes before my husband appeared.

"I spent the next two hours learning how to make watermelon whales and apple birds and came home with a smashing vegetable centerpiece.

"As I walked through the door, Danny came speeding across the room on roller blades, almost knocking my creation out of my hands. Three of the neighbors' children had joined the crowd. No one had done any homework. No one was sleeping, and my husband wasn't home.

"Just then the phone rang. I thought that maybe it was my husband and so I ran to get it.

"'Hello. Is this Mrs. Henig?' the man asked, mispronouncing my name. 'Yes,' I answered wearily.

"I knew who it was. Every night, without fail, the same

thing happens. Different telemarketers each time, but always persistent.

"'Hello, can I speak to Mrs. Henig?' They can't seem to get 'Hoenig' right. Then the story is always similar. 'Would you like to refinance your mortgage? Avail yourself of our new credit card? Are you interested in a chance-of-a-lifetime investment?' Tonight I had less patience than usual to listen to the sales pitch.

"Once I affirmed my identity, he went at it, 'Mrs. Henig, may I speak to you for a few moments?'

"My son had switched on the popcorn machine and apparently then walked away without providing a bowl to catch the popping kernels. Holding the receiver, I watched the popcorn explode in every direction.

"'No, you may not,' I snapped impatiently and let the phone drop into the cradle, as I grabbed a fruit bowl, dumped out the apples and raced towards the spluttering machine. I was not proud of myself, but at that moment it was the best I wanted to do."

Anne stopped her narration for a minute to let the lesson sink in. I got it.

Wise, caring Anne had slammed the phone down on someone! I was listening. I was hearing what she was obviously trying to tell me. If *she* could do that, then anyone could. And my dear, considerate friend was nonetheless normal and decent.

It was a powerful story for me, which I never would have grasped without her personal experience to illustrate.

"The next day in school," Anne continued, "one of my students handed me a note." (Anne is a sixth grade home economics teacher.)

"It was addressed to me.

> *"My daughter Dahlia gave me a note, which was signed by you. You asked me to call you. I called last night. You yelled into the phone and hung up. I think I will bring this to the attention of the principal.*
>
> *Signed,*
> *Mr. Zolnick (Dahlia's father, in case you don't know.)"*

"That's it. That's my first story," Anne declared dolefully. "Which story would you like to hear next? Where my husband was that evening? Why it took me nine-and-a-half hours to return your call? Or where I applied for a new teaching position?"

Was she joking? I would have asked, but my mind was elsewhere. It had reverted back to the morning. Now, it occurred to me that when a neighbor puts the phone down like that, wouldn't a *normal, decent* person be concerned if all was OK in that house, instead of wasting a whole morning and afternoon being angry?

If we are not able to figure it out ourselves, talking it over with someone else can help, especially someone with wisdom and insight, who can give us a new perspective and help us view an unfathomable situation from a different angle.

35.

The Day of Judgment

This past Rosh Hashanah I went together with my brother-in-law to his synagogue. When I walked in on the first night, I immediately noticed a sign in large bold letters firmly requesting that no children be brought unless they are old enough to participate in the service.

Imagine my surprise the next day when someone sitting one row in front of me brought five children with him — all equipped with bags of nosh. They were not especially noisy, but neither were they just sitting quietly, and the younger ones were certainly not able to follow the service.

After going through half of the service feeling a bit annoyed, I realized that on Rosh Hashanah of all days, when we ask the Almighty to judge us favorably, I should do the same.

I thought for a few minutes before coming to the conclusion that probably their mother was not feeling well — maybe she even had a high fever — and so the father had no choice but to bring the children along with him.

So leave them with a neighbor, or a babysitter. I'm sure

if you thought a bit, you could have arranged something. Why drag them to a place they don't belong? With all my good intentions, I was having a hard time absolving that father.

I eyed them now and again and then tried to concentrate on my prayer book.

It was at the end of the service that they caught my attention once more, when they stood up, in unison. Believe me, there was hardly a dry eye in sight as those five kids of gradational heights started to say *Kaddish*. It was the man seated next to me who told me it was for their mother who had passed away a few months before.

❧

Even when we rise to the occasion and offer the "offender" a favorable judgment, we may have come up with a defense that only partially clears him. While that is also commendable, we should consider that he may deserve even more.

36.

Vacuous Vapors

It started like this. Our neighbor, Josh Reznick, who also happens to be my husband's business partner, is in and out of our house all the time. When his daughter came down with croup, he asked to borrow our cold-air vaporizer, which he had seen us use on many occasions. It took weeks until they finally returned it, but I did not mind. I was just happy their daughter was feeling better.

Two weeks later, our baby developed a severe cough. The doctor recommended that we try using a vaporizer in her room. We used it for two nights, and when I plugged it in on the third evening, it would not start. I took off the top and saw that the motor was not turning. On closer inspection, I noticed that the bottom area was covered with mineral deposits. I did not recall it ever looking like that. Then I realized what had happened. When *we* use it, we always empty out the water when the machine is off, as it states in the directions for those who live in an area with hard water, as we do. I had mentioned this to our neighbors, the Reznicks, but just in passing. I did not stress it. I should have written it on the vaporizer so they would have had to remember. They obviously forgot, and the motor must have stopped because of the interference of the deposits.

We needed that vaporizer for our baby, so I was annoyed at their negligence and for the inconvenience they were causing us. I immediately brought the defective part to a reliable repairman in town. He could not fix it on the spot, but he looked at it quickly to give me an estimate. Sure enough, he confirmed my suspicions.

"Most probably," he said, "you did not empty the water after each use, and the motor became jammed because of the sedimentation. Most of the vaporizers I repair are brought in for just this reason."

Well, what he said was only partially true, because we had not left it in the water — it was the neighbors! Now that my suspicions had been confirmed, my annoyance grew. My husband tried to calm me, but I was still upset that I had to pay for *their* oversight. True, I was partially at fault for not having emphasized the point about the water. But, I reasoned, if people borrow an electrical appliance, they should make sure to find out how to use it properly and listen carefully when instructions are being given.

When Josh came over that evening, I discreetly encouraged my husband to mention it to him. Maybe he would at least want to share the cost of the repair. (Although who knew if it was even repairable or would ever work again?) I was working myself up into a temper, but my husband was reluctant to say anything to his partner.

What should I do? I decided to calm down. My baby was getting better even without the vaporizer. Let me be satisfied with the lesson I learned from this: When lending out electrical appliances, be careful to give specific instructions.

A few days later I went to town to pick up the piece. The repairman was happy to tell me that it was only a minor repair, and he gave me the bill. Then he added, almost as an afterthought, "Part of the motor had jammed. Looks to me like someone dropped it."

"Oh," I said in a half whisper.

I felt like I was dreaming. This could not be true.

Then the scene came back to me. Josh returned the vaporizer. I put it down on a shelf. But I did not set it down properly, and a minute later, it fell with a crash to the floor. I ran over to see if there was damage. All was fine; no crack, no break. I plugged it in. I heard the whir of the motor. I let out a sigh of relief and put it back in its place.

My thoughts returned to the present. A little shaky, I took the vaporizer, thanked the man, and walked out.

On the way to the car, my brain was churning, trying to sort this out. Could it be possible that the motor would run for two days until the damage done to it by the fall jammed it so it couldn't run anymore?

I slid behind the wheel, still overcome by the turn of events.

I was so sure *they* had caused it. It had seemed like the evidence was crystal clear. Even the repairman had initially confirmed my conclusion, and I never remember the machine having so much sedimentation. Unless it was there before and I never noticed it? And anyway, could sedimentation build up so quickly in just a few weeks?

Then the thought came to me, if the repairman had absentmindedly forgotten to mention his second evaluation and I had been left with his first assumption, I would always have had a "case" against the Reznicks.

I am humbled. I'm ashamed that I indicted our friends, with such confidence, and thankful that at least my husband had not said anything to them.

I thought I had learned the lesson intended: Never lend without giving explicit instructions. That is an important lesson. I just never dreamed there would be more to learn from a vaporizer; in particular that my solidly built charges could evaporate like illusory, intangible vapors.

Of course, we are right. Not even a small doubt remains in our minds that the other side is wrong, plain and simple, at fault.

How embarrassing when we discover the truth, and as we pass a mirror, we see that culprit staring us straight in the face.

37.
Cold Cuts

A friend of mine bought a salami at her local grocery store. After opening it she discovered that it wasn't fresh, and she decided to return it.

To her dismay, the grocery owner refused to accept it, telling her that she should contact the manufacturer directly. He explained that if he gave her the refund he would lose money on the deal, whereas she would gain if she phoned.

Initially, my friend was annoyed at the grocer for trying to avoid a responsibility she felt was his, for the excuses he gave, and the bother she anticipated having with the manufacturer.

Given no choice, she called anyway. To her amazement, immediately upon hearing her complaint, the salami manufacturer asked for her address, and promptly delivered a huge supply of assorted processed meat to her door.

It then occurred to her that the grocery owner had advised her correctly.

Giving a person the benefit of the doubt does not always come easily, but, as we see here, it pays off.

38.

Getting into Hot Soup

My Aunt Rose was visiting from out of state and invited our whole family out to dinner at the nicest restaurant in town.

On the one hand, it was a real treat. How often do we go out to eat, and at such a "ritzy" place, no less. On the other hand, this would take some careful planning. I made a mental to-do list: Get everyone bathed and dressed to suit the occasion, give the kids a quick review of table manners followed by a summary of restaurant decorum, and warn them not to take advantage of Aunt Rose's generosity.

So there we were. The waiter formally handed everyone a menu. Those who knew enough to discern which side was up were thrown by the variety of choices, not to mention the foreign words. Meanwhile, I delicately attempted to steer the children towards the more modest selections.

Ordering turned out to be no simple matter. Everyone changed his mind at least three times. Finally the orders were in, and I was settling back in my chair to enjoy the ambience, when out of the blue my teenage daughter Shari requested soup. "Why?" I asked, not hiding my displeasure. "That's an extra and quite unnecessary."

But Aunt Rose interrupted, "Soup is fine and healthy." I was not convinced — not at six dollars a cup!

While we waited, the children entertained Aunt Rose with stories I never even knew they knew. The time passed pleasantly, and before long the waiter brought the dinners. Once we sorted out what went to whom, everyone dug in. I had decided not to order for myself. I figured what the younger ones could not handle would be more than enough for me, hoping in this way to trim the bill a bit.

Everything was running smoothly when I felt a tug at my sleeve and heard that same teenager whisper, "Ma, I don't want to finish my soup."

More boiling than the soup, I answered this usually reasonable girl, "I'll finish it," meanwhile shooting her a look of exasperation which relayed my message: "It's enough you ordered it, but to leave it over is unpardonable."

Reviewing the evening at home, considering what could have been, I must say that all had gone well. But now was the time and place to say something to my daughter. She is old enough to understand, especially at such prices, that we only order what we can handle. I gave her my little speech, and she answered me quietly saying, "But Mom, I saw that you didn't order. I knew you were hungry, and I figured if I said I didn't want the soup, you would answer your usual, 'Okay, I'll take it.'"

My daughter — who does us proud with her ingenious solutions and bright ideas — came through once again.

This was not the first time in my child-raising career that I took to the podium, delivering a fire and brimstone speech, only to discover that I was talking to the wrong audience.

❧

As parents, we have a duty to correct our children. If we judge them favorably and whitewash negative actions, how can we hope to guide them to improve their character?

When we see our children behaving inappropriately, judging favorably is the first step. Once we consider the possibility that we might be misunderstanding their intentions or missing information, our attitude towards them will be more positive. Sensing our fairness, they will be more apt to accepting our rebuke, if it is still in store.

Giving children the benefit of the doubt can only improve our role as educators.

39.

I've Got My Eye on You

If people are already coming out on a cold winter's night to hear a lecture, why don't they listen?

That is what I was thinking that evening as I presented my lecture, one of a series on the topic of medieval Jewish history. Fifteen minutes earlier, two women had walked in (about ten minutes after we had started) and sat down in the back row. That was fine, as all the other seats were filled. What was not fine was that from the minute they sat down they did not stop talking. It's true, they were speaking quietly, and I could not hear them, but it was nonetheless distracting for me, as the lecturer, to know that they had so little interest in what I had to say that they were not prepared to stop gabbing for one minute!

I pushed these thoughts away so I could concentrate on the material.

Three-quarters of an hour later I finished. And so, finally, did these two ladies. Gathering my notes and preparing to leave, I noticed the pair approaching me.

At least they have the decency to come and apologize, I thought. But their apology was far from the one I expected.

"Thank you so much, Professor Frankel. We really enjoyed your talk," one of them said.

I did a double take.

"And we learned so much," she added enthusiastically.

Come on now. She has to be kidding!

"I'd like to introduce myself. And this is my sister," she continued. "We are sorry we showed up late. We usually try to come early and take seats in the front row. But because of the rain, we had to drive slowly, so we were a few minutes late. You probably did not notice, but as you were speaking, I was repeating what you were saying. My sister is hearing impaired, but she reads lips very well. That's why the front row, where she can see you, is best for her..."

We may ask, "Why don't people explain themselves? If they would, then we would not have to exert ourselves to find merit."

One possibility is that there is no time, as in the story above.

Even if there had been time, it may not occur to the "guilty party" that his actions warrant explanation.

Especially when we are absorbed in a worthy pursuit, we are not alert to the fact that our well-meant endeavor could have a second interpretation.

Still another insight is that when we personally have never been on that "other side" (in this case, at the podium), we are often not aware of what could be disturbing in that situation. When we are unaware that our behavior is amiss, no explanation or apology can be expected to follow.

Why don't people explain themselves?

Above are just a few of the many possible answers.

40

Duped

"OK, OK! If she wants me to go so much, I'll just go already!"

Realizing that I was at it again, I looked warily over my shoulder to see if anyone had heard me. Having suffered frequent teasing over my new habit of talking to myself, I was anticipating another quip, but to my relief no one was around. I quickly finished putting the groceries away and went to phone my sister.

For two weeks she had been calling me to go with her to a newly discovered store. "I know you'll love it," she cajoled. "They have famous brand names at great prices." She sounded just like an advertisement.

My sister knew what to say to convince me. But that was only the first step. The second was to find a time to suit the both of us. When she was free, I had to do carpool. When I was available, she had an aerobics class. And with both of us working at part-time jobs — of course at different hours — we just could not get our act together.

We finally arranged a tentative time. Now we just had to

work out the logistics of which children to take along and who would babysit for the others.

At the appointed time (add half an hour for the usual delays) we were off. It was a pleasant ride with a minimum clash of arms in the back seat.

Having found parking right near the store, we emerged from the car and proceeded towards Childrenswear House. As usual, my sister was right. Ten minutes of browsing confirmed that despite the small size of the store, the selection was large, the quality was good, and pleasantly surprising price tags abounded. Not one to buy what I do not need even when the price is right, I did not expect to make a big haul. Nonetheless, I did end up choosing a few things: Two pairs of pants from a well-known manufacturer for my nine-year-old and a wrinkle-proof skirt and top for my seven-year-old (just the style all her friends have, she claimed). My sister told me that the lightweight tights in this store were top quality, so I took two pairs.

By then the kids had just about had it. My sister, who had also managed to pick up a few things, agreed that we should not push our luck, so we went to the register to ring up our purchases. Bags in hands, we counted heads, piled into the car, and headed home. As we were riding, I had the feeling that I had better check the receipt. Somehow it had not turned out as cheap as I had expected it to.

When I got home, I took out the receipt and went over

each item: two pairs of pants at thirteen dollars each; one outfit size eight, twenty-five dollars; two pairs of tights, nine dollars each. I did a double take. Good quality is good quality, but nine dollars for a pair of tights in a discount store is ludicrous. I do not know how I had overlooked that in the store, but I felt good knowing that I had caught this one in time. (Luckily, I had not opened the packages.)

I made it my business to get back to the shop the next day before the owner could give me any problems about returning too late.

"So, what do you think? Was it a mistake?" There I was again, talking to myself. This time I was alone in the car, so I continued conversing with the windshield. "Or is that the way this guy makes a living? Marking down prices and then making up for it with a 'mistake' at the cash register. That's a naughty thought," I told myself, "but there *are* swindlers in the world, aren't there?"

Parking was more difficult this time, but eventually, I found a spot. I jumped out, determined to keep this confrontation pleasant.

The owner was alone at the register, so at least there would not be a public scene. I walked up and told him there had been a mistake with my purchase the day before. I had it all there in the bag, the pants, the outfit, and the tights. I showed him the items and the bill. "Surely you're not charging eighteen dollars for two pairs of children's tights,"

I said, pointing to the two closed packages.

He looked at me but did not respond. He simply pointed to the package of tights which I had placed on the counter in front of him. My eyes followed his finger resting on the top right-hand corner of the package. There, in blue letters, not too large (but not too small either), was printed "three in a package."

We are not disregarding cases of real dishonesty, but there are many suspicious situations that a little investigation would reveal as innocent. While we are obligated to protect ourselves from loss or damage, we must also be wary of falsely accusing others.

It is unfair to transform an innocent occurrence into a malicious act. Giving the benefit of the doubt forces us to consider the distinction.

41.

The Mad Uncle

About five years ago my grandfather, of blessed memory, passed away. Although I missed the funeral, I was told the following story at the *shivah*:

At the funeral, my grandfather's brother-in-law, Uncle Aaron, a very respected and humble individual, announced that the deceased specifically requested in his will that if eulogies were given, they should be brief. Uncle Aaron therefore urged all those who were delivering eulogies to make them as brief as possible.

The speakers described my grandfather's laudable character and actions, but kept their words succinct. Everyone adhered to my uncle's request and delivered their respective thoughts briefly. Everyone, that is, except for Uncle Aaron himself!

Between every eulogy, he spoke at length, ignoring his own plea for brevity. The funeral ended up taking much longer than funerals take, and many people left muttering to each other about the chutzpah the brother-in-law had displayed. Not only did he not practice what he preached, but he also blatantly ignored the wishes of the deceased!

At the *shivah,* my father asked his uncle to explain. Knowing him as a man of integrity, he felt he must have had a good reason for his bizarre behavior. His answer stunned us.

While the first eulogy was being delivered — after he had just made the announcement to keep things short — Uncle Aaron was told by the burial society (*chevrah kaddisha*) that the caretakers of the cemetery take a lunch break between 1:00 and 3:00 in the afternoon. Since the funeral had started close to noon and the cemetery was a forty-minute drive away, it would have been impossible to make it there before one o'clock. That being so, the funeral procession would arrive at the cemetery with no one there to assist with the burial. The body would be waiting to be buried for an hour and a half. So, because of respect for the deceased (*kavod hameis*), Uncle Aaron decided to prolong the funeral as much as possible. He felt that honoring the deceased was more important than what people would say about him for ignoring his own request. And sure enough, the procession arrived at the cemetery just as the caretakers came back from their lunch break.

❧

Would you have chosen this option? Maybe not. But the importance of the story is not whether we agree with a person's decisions and evaluations. Rather, its significance is in teaching us once again to consider that there may be, as the expression goes, "a method to his madness."

42.

Shedding Pounds – and Suspicions

We had taken a new route that morning, more rugged than the one we were used to. The heat and the hills made our outing a bit challenging, but sticking to our exercise routine was important to both of us, so we carried plenty of water and put the weather behind us.

Hannah and I have been walking partners for the last two years. We feel more energized than we have in years and are proud of our consistency. Besides all the health benefits, we love each other's company.

It is not only our morning excursions that have knitted our friendship. We are also both very involved in our community organization, which assists individuals and families in need. Those needs come in many shapes and forms, and so does our response. We have volunteers to transport people to hospitals and doctor appointments. There is a committee that does grocery shopping and various errands for the homebound. We keep lists of community members who can be called upon to visit hospital patients, nursing home residents, or those laid up in their own homes. And we even provide an emergency babysitting service. What's that, you ask? You know, you are ready to leave when the babysitter asks to cancel! Just contact us and we'll help you out.

One of the most beneficial services we offer is providing home-cooked food for the recuperating. These meals are delivered, for example, to those who are ailing, bedridden, post-operative, after birth, or elderly. For most recipients, these meals are lifesavers.

That Friday morning, we were trudging up and down those hills, when we spotted Gabriella Simon's home. Gabriella has been on our list for three weeks now, following an accident in her home. She had been looking for something on a high shelf and had climbed up on a chair with wheels. "It was just for a second" (those famous last words), and for a split second, is it worth taking time to start looking for something sturdier? When the chair started rolling, she took a nasty fall and has been flat on her back ever since.

We entered the scene as soon as we learned of Gabriella's misfortune. Besides taking care of meals, we made sure the house was running smoothly. It was a big undertaking, but that's what we're there for. I shouldn't say "besides meals," as if it's an incidental service. Far from it. Each day our volunteer cook prepares a hot three-course dinner, which is specially personalized for the needs of Gabriella's family.

As we neared the Simons' home, we were met with the distinct aroma of freshly baked challahs. Our eyes met. Without a word, each knew what the other was thinking: *It's Friday morning. Why is someone baking in a home where everything that is needed will be delivered in the afternoon?* As we walked past the house, I wondered if Hannah also detected the aroma of chicken soup cooking.

We had about ten minutes to go before it was time to turn back. Walking briskly, we debated whether it was more *our* responsibility to keep on top of Gabriella's progress, or whether it was up to *her* to let us know when she no longer needed our services. Was there a chance that she could be taking unfair advantage of the goodness of the community?

On the way back we passed the Simons' home again. Just then the door opened, and a woman carrying a large cardboard box stepped out. She nodded in our direction and smiled. Hannah recognized her as one of Gabriella's neighbors. She stopped a minute to say hello, and we both could see (and smell) that the box was full of freshly cooked food and baked goods. Not wanting to appear nosy, I did not question her, but she volunteered the information herself.

"Yesterday, my stove broke down," she explained. "The repairman said he could not come before Monday. I was on the way to Solly's Take-Out, when I passed Gabriella's house. I remembered that she is out of commission and would not be using her stove. I asked her if she would mind me 'borrowing' her kitchen — I promised to leave it spotless. With her ready consent I started cooking last night and came back this morning to finish up." With a tired smile on her face, she headed for her car where she deposited her cardboard box.

❧

We only know of this story because someone opened a door. But how many thousands of incidents of reproach never become "stories," because the door of understanding remained shut.

Let such stories spur us on so that when we encounter behavior that appears to us questionable, inappropriate, or worse, we will be willing to pry open doors of insight and discernment. Even if they are stuck and require a bit of determination to unlatch, we must be willing to tug.

43.

One for the Books

Pushing back my chair, I stood up, bounced up and down on my feet a few times, and shook my head back and forth, attempting to shake off the stiffness that had built up as I sat hunched over my papers for three hours. A page full of doodles danced in front of me, testifying to my predicament. I had clearly hit a snag. In the middle of a research project and pressed for time, I was stymied. Until I would get this point clarified, there was no way to move ahead.

Sluggishly, I walked around the room and then over to the window, hoping that the view would offer me some new inspiration. I was right on target, because, after a few minutes of staring at my chestnut tree, an idea popped into my head. About three weeks before, I had come across an ad for a newly published book that dealt with the exact topic I was working on. The name of the book escaped me, but if I could only get my hands on it now, I would stand a chance of sorting this thing out.

No doubt, lacking a title put me at a disadvantage. In spite of that, it was possible that some obliging bookstore would willingly help me out. If so, it was worth a few calls.

I flipped through the yellow pages, and started calling the bookstore listings, alphabetically. Much to my relief, The Book Stop, the second name down, proved to be my salvation. The man who answered the phone figured out from my description which book I meant, and immediately went to check if they had it. Calculating that it was already too late to get there before closing time, the salesman tried to be helpful and told me they opened every day at 9:00. If I wanted, he would put the book aside for me. I calculated that if I got there first thing in the morning, I would manage to pick up my book and still make it on time to my 9:30 class.

Traffic was lighter than usual, so by 8:40 I had already reached my destination. I found parking and then walked back the two blocks towards The Book Stop. It was about a quarter to nine, which left me with no choice but to wait. Spotting a bus stop bench in front of the store, I took out my newspaper and sat down to read.

A minute later, a lanky young man, wearing a checked jacket and brown cap, approached The Book Stop and knocked at the door. Not receiving an immediate response, he banged again louder.

I was on the verge of calling out, "Calm down, there's still fifteen minutes 'til opening. Can't you read the sign?" Instead, I read my own sign, "Mind your own business," which I try to post in front of my nose at times like this.

Let me tell you, this fellow was persistent, and a bit impatient, too. His banging was making a big racket. Not making headway at the door, he walked over to the side where there was a window, and started rapping on the glass.

He must need a book even more desperately than I do, I thought, sympathizing with his plight. *Maybe he's late for a class, too.*

Not taking no for an answer, he then returned to the door and pounded even harder.

What makes people tick? As a sociology major, people watching never ceases to fascinate me. Most probably the lanky customer saw the posted sign with store hours just as I did. So what was going through his mind as he hammered on that door well before opening time? Maybe he felt that if the owners realized how desperate he was, they would consider doing him the favor of opening a little earlier. That's a possibility. Maybe he had tried the same tactic at other times in other places and it had worked.

Sure enough, the door opened and a heavyset man stuck out his head. Watching this scene, my brain let out a signal. *If they're making an exception for him, I'm going in too!* I thought optimistically, jumping up. As I was bounding for the door, the lanky man exchanged a word with the proprietor and was let in.

I know the owner saw me, because I ran fast and was standing right there when he closed the door in my face.

That's right — just slammed it in my face!

Why is he better than me? You made one exception, so now make a second one.

Seeing that persistence paid off, I decided to try it too. I knocked. And then louder. No response.

I reviewed the other man's strategy and decided to follow it. I went to the window and banged. A face appeared from behind a curtain and mouthed, "Ten more minutes."

"But," I mouthed back, which is all I got to say before the curtain dropped. What I had wanted to add was, *You let him in. Give me a break. I'm also in a hurry.* In any case, I was not given a chance to present my plea.

Cool down, I admonished myself. *OK, so it's not fair. Don't work yourself up over ten minutes.*

At 9:01 the stocky man finally opened the door. I had been knocking steadily for a full minute already and was tempted to continue knocking — on his face. Instead, I just gave him a disgusted look as I walked past.

It was then that I spotted the man in the checked jacket and brown cap, standing next to the cash register behind the counter.

Take my word for it, the person to whom this happened is just as clever as you. Then why didn't he figure it out (like you might have)?

As a rule, when we are thinking in a certain direction, other possibilities simply do not occur to us, unless we consciously train ourselves to judge others with favor, or are naturally inclined in that direction. For most of us, at that moment of frustration or censure, there is only one, foregone, conclusion. We are so focused on our one path of thought, we never consider that there might be an alternate route to the same place, another explanation that will solve our dilemma.

This is true even when the other explanation is reasonable, maybe even more credible, and in actuality is more frequently the case.

44.

The Hearing Test

Restless. I guess that is how you might describe me as I sat in the doctor's office. I had recently been through a battery of tests and was more than a bit anxious as I waited for the results. I was sitting on one side of the desk playing with a loose thread on my sweater, the doctor on the other side, pressing computer keys trying to locate my file. The seconds that passed felt like an eternity.

The doctor seemed to be getting nowhere. I watched her every move, feeling the tension building up in my neck. Then the doctor leaned forward, her eyes focused intently on the screen. "What's this? Something's not right."

My heart started to pound so loudly I was sure the doctor could hear it, but she never once looked in my direction, her eyes remaining focused intently on the screen.

Maybe I misunderstood, I warned myself.

But the next moment I heard the doctor again. "Something is definitely irregular. This time it looks serious."

I closed my eyes. An overwhelming weakness settled over me. I sat in my chair, digesting her words.

Stay calm, I commanded myself. *You can't go to pieces here in the office.*

I heard her chair move. I opened my eyes and watched as the doctor stood up. "I have to get someone to check this right now," and she walked out.

Alone in the room, I was finding it hard to breathe. How long did I sit there? I cannot tell you, but eventually the door opened and the doctor walked in together with a man wearing a white coat and a stethoscope around his neck. The two of them sat down at the desk. They scanned the screen, punched some keys, and exchanged a few words I could not hear. Then the second doctor turned to the first and announced glumly, "You're right."

Confirmation. *Just give me the strength to get through this,* I prayed.

From behind my closed eyes, I heard the doctor continue, "Something isn't right. There must be a problem with the computer, and this time it does look like it's more serious than the last time."

Although the shock and fright of the last few minutes still engulfed me, the nightmare was over. The doctor then remembered that a patient was sitting in front of her. She turned to me. "You can go. Everything is normal," she said matter-of-factly.

"Is my hearing also normal?" I shot out sharply. The doctor looked at me quizzically.

With as much control as I could muster at that moment, I continued, "If you believe I can hear, then you also know that I heard what you were saying. Why didn't you consider the effect of your words? How did you think I would understand things like, 'something's irregular' or 'this time it looks serious,' coming from a doctor who is supposed to be evaluating my test results?"

The doctor closed my file and said impassively, "I'm an internist, not a psychiatrist."

❧

Wasn't it obvious that the doctor was referring to a technical problem on the computer? It is surely easier to see the incident as "obvious" when one is not that anxious patient.

Is there anything to say on the doctor's behalf, either for her statements in front of the computer or for her curt reply? When intentions are benign, even people in responsible positions may be unaware how offensive their behavior appears.

Still, after hearing the patient's reaction, why didn't this doctor apologize? Truth be told, don't most of us have difficulty admitting a mistake, let alone apologizing for it? Reaction to criticism is usually defensive even for professionals. Although this does not totally exonerate the doc-

tor's behavior, the exercise of judging favorably asks us to consider even a partial defense.

Some would still argue that the doctor's behavior was inexcusable. The question is, would they say the same about their own mistakes? The term we use for others is "inexcusable." When it comes to ourselves, for the same mistake we might say: "I usually wouldn't do that," "It was the end of a hard day," "Afterwards, I realized I was wrong," It was partially her fault too."

Instinctively, we know to defend ourselves. It always takes a studied effort to do the same for others.

45.

Acquire a Friend, and Judge Him with Favor

(Ethics of the Fathers, 1:6)

Last summer, my father changed jobs, and we had to move to another city. That meant we all would be entering new schools in the fall.

Even before we finished unpacking, my little brother had already found a friend on the block who would be in his class. By the time school started in September, I still did not have a friend in my grade, and I was really worried about being the new girl in the class.

It turned out that my worries were unnecessary. On the first day of school, I sat next to a girl named Miri. She was friendly and helpful, explaining all those things a new student needs to know. She made sure to include me in all the games, and we became best friends. Now we always walk home from school together and help each other with homework. If I am ever sick, she calls me to fill me in on what we learned that day, and to cheer me up. And I always do the same for her.

One day I woke up with a fever and had to stay home. I slept late that morning and only got up when my mother came in with some tea. The day dragged on. I couldn't wait until school was over and Miri would call.

I kept watching the clock and waiting and waiting. Every time the phone rang, I listened impatiently for my mother to call my name. Each time that it was not for me, my disappointment grew.

Soon it was suppertime. I still had not heard from my friend. Why didn't she call? I was tempted to pick up the phone and call her, but I was too upset.

After a while I decided I had to speak to her. After three rings, she picked up and said hello. Without waiting a second, I blurted out, "I'm sick. Why didn't you call me?"

For a second, Miri did not answer. Then I heard her voice. Only then did I notice that it sounded low and hoarse, and a little hurt. "Call you? I was waiting for you to call me. I was also sick today."

It happens with little folks, and not less with grown-ups. So often, the real reason for delay, absence, or disappointments of all sizes, is illness. Contemplate the following:

while we often use illness as an excuse to explain our own behavior, we do not suppose or allow that excuse for others. More ironic is that even at the very moment I am ailing, the farthest thing from my mind is considering that you may be too.

46

How Could That Be?

It is funny how certain scenes from the past remain with us. I imagine many of us can remember a word or encounter that was pivotal, a fork in the road that gently or not so gently drove us to the left or right, down one path of life or another.

When I was eleven years old, my mother came home from a parent-teacher meeting at my Hebrew School. I was a good student and got along well with the teacher, possibly because my interest surpassed the rest of the class, most of whom did not want to be there in the first place. The information fascinated me, and when Mrs. Benedict taught, I felt she was talking directly to me.

I had waited up, in anticipation of those all too important words of praise and encouragement that we all need and crave at any age. As soon as the front door opened, I jumped up and ran over to greet my mother. She seemed calm and content, greeting me with a smile and a hug. My lips curled up into a satisfied grin as Mom quoted the teacher, who had praised me for my faultless attendance and interest in her lessons. So you can understand that I was really not prepared for what came next, when Mom went on to say that the teacher was disappointed in me.

I felt like a bucket of cold water had been thrown in my face. Disappointed? Why? How could that be? Instantly, I turned away so that my mother would not see my eyes filling with tears. What can I tell you — I was crushed. Meanwhile, my mom was distracted by something, and she walked away. I took advantage of the interruption and escaped to my room. Neither of us brought up the conversation again, and the matter ended there.

I never went back to Hebrew School. My parents begged and bribed me to go, or at least to explain my sudden refusal to go, but to no avail. I was hurt and confused because I had always been an "A" student. Humiliation prevented me from facing my teacher. Sensitive, oversensitive, or pre-adolescent, call it what you will, but that was the way it was, and that was the way my Jewish education ended.

Twenty years later, I was studying in a seminary in Jerusalem, rediscovering my roots. Somewhere a door had opened and beckoned me back down a road I had turned away from two decades before. I picked up with the same enthusiasm, the same eagerness to soak up new information about my rich heritage that had come to an abrupt halt 20 years earlier.

During that time I returned to the States to visit my folks.

One morning over coffee and sugar doughnuts, my mother and I were discussing the Middle East, Jerusalem, Judaism, and life in general. Mom wanted to know more about what they taught in seminary and what had brought me there. Without too much forethought, I heard myself saying, "Imagine if Mrs. Benedict could see me now. She'd be shocked!" I laughed, licking the sugar from my fingertips.

"Why 'shocked'?" my mother asked, apparently surprised at my choice of expression.

Memories of that evening of long ago floated back. With a lot less emotion, I was able to tell Mom about my reaction to Mrs. Benedict's disappointment in me. My mother's response turned *me* into the shocked one.

"Oh, Julie, that wasn't at all what she meant. How could you think that? She loved you. You were her favorite student. What she said was that she was disappointed in your late start in Hebrew School (I only started at age nine), because she felt you had such potential for success. When you dropped out, she kept calling me, begging me to convince you to come back."

It amazed me to think that because of that one misunderstood statement, my life had taken a different direction. Maybe the phone rang in the middle of my mother's sentence, or the dryer buzzer went off. Whatever it was, it took me twenty years to discover that I had walked out on a conversation that had never been finished.

Missing parts of a conversation can be at the root of hard feelings. At times we arrive in the middle of discussions and do not realize we missed the beginning. And other times it's the tail end that escapes us. We are constantly involved in verbal give-and-take, and boundaries of each and every topic are often ill-defined. When words hurt, one way to judge others with more favor is to consider the possibility of not having heard all there was to say.

47.

Dental Assistance

Nat Besser and I met on the 7:23 to Grand Central. We both sat in the third row of the second car, in front of an executive who made a daily conference call on his cellular phone to his colleagues in Hong Kong. Behind us were two commuters who routinely exchanged day-trading tips and then dozed off for the rest of the ride. Nat and I, both garrulous by nature, struck up a conversation, and over time we became good friends.

He got off one stop before me, where he had his dental practice. I heard that it was quite an operation, with several associates sharing an impressive office. Nat Besser was earning a solid living and a fine reputation as a dentist.

So when my wife Tamara had a run-in with her dentist, I suggested that she switch to Besser.

One morning, after the usual chitchat — How's business? How are the kids? — I broached the subject. Sincerely apologizing, Nat explained that he was so overloaded, his secretary had been turning people away for months. Especially now that the office was in the midst of moving to a new location, it would be impossible. I joked about being afraid to go home to my wife with a refusal. My pal must have taken me seriously, because before getting off the train, he made a comment about checking with his secretary, Mrs. Willoughby, about cancellations.

Sure enough, the next day, Nat — true to his word — announced that he had caught Mrs. Willoughby in a good mood, so if my wife would call the office, she had promised to fit her in. Tamara called and was given an appointment the following week.

After the initial visit, my wife was told she needed more extensive treatment and was scheduled for three more appointments. By this time his office had relocated. Nat was no longer riding on my train, but my wife continued bringing me regards. His reputation for professional competence was confirmed and reconfirmed.

When the work was completed and we still had not been billed, I asked my secretary to call and get the amount due. Mrs. Willoughby did not seem to have it recorded and asked if we wanted to speak to Dr. Besser directly. When Besser got on, my secretary explained that my wife had not been billed. Could he tell us the amount owed so that we could send a check? Besser's reply was, "Well, why doesn't she call herself?" Baffled, she hung up disturbed, not exactly sure what his response meant or what hers should have been.

"Could you repeat that?" I asked my secretary when she

came in to give me the message. I heard it again, but it made no sense to me either. I couldn't understand the problem. All I wanted was to pay the bill. What's the big deal about giving me the amount? Shaking my head in bewilderment, I watched my secretary, who was also at a loss, shrug as she closed the door behind her.

When I arrived home that evening, I told my wife what had happened. We were both stumped. Nat was such a nice, pleasant guy. Not at all difficult. Something did not fit.

The following Sunday my in-laws dropped by. My father-in-law is a retired orthodontist. As a former member of the medical profession, maybe he would understand Besser's strange message. I figured I would tell him what happened and hear what he had to say.

"It's simple," he replied and went on to explain what he thought anyone could figure out.

He got it right on the first try.

How do I know? Because Monday morning Tamara reached Besser. Thanking him again, she apologized for letting things ride and asked to be billed.

Nat apologized for the run-around. Confirming my father-in-law's guess, he explained that he was giving us a special price that he preferred to quote directly.

Unfavorable judgments come in all sizes. There are those actions and statements that appear so grossly unreasonable, they leave us shaking or shocked. More frequently, we are caught up in smaller judgment calls involving issues of lesser gravity.

The willingness to judge people with favor includes the many unremarkable instances, the minor irritations that occur throughout our day, like the story above, when we indignantly call on the carpet some people who may not deserve that invitation.

48.

A Bakery Turnover

I was standing in line at our local bakery, waiting impatiently for the man in front of me to make his choice. He kept vacillating between the coffee cake and the apple strudel and was holding up not only me, but a long line of harried customers behind me. This was probably not an unfamiliar scene for the saleslady and she remained unfazed. The strudel finally won, and he handed the clerk the money. She passed his package over the counter with the change, and I moved up to take his place.

"I'll have a rye bread and a pound of those cookies," I requested, pointing to the chocolate chip cookies in the display case below.

When I looked up, I realized she was not even listening to what I had said. Looking straight ahead, she was shaking her head, a troubled expression on her face. She was definitely disturbed about something, and I had a feeling it had nothing to do with chocolate chips.

A second later, with her eyes riveted on the exit, she blurted out, "Do you realize what that man has done?" obviously referring to the man before me who had just walked off. "Do you know what he has done to completely innocent people? Do you have any idea how many people he has cheated?" she continued vehemently.

Oh no, I thought. I had recognized that man from our community. I did not know much about him, but thanks to her, *now* I did.

Why did she have to tell me that? How does she know it's even true? Now, every time I see him....

I looked at the salesclerk with disdain. I wanted to let her know how I felt about her gossiping, but once again she was not paying any attention to me. She had shifted positions and now seemed to be concentrating on the news broadcast from the radio on the shelf nearby. Preoccupied, I hadn't even heard its dry drone until this minute.

Finally, the clerk turned her attention back to me and resumed her tirade.

"How low can people be? Doesn't that man have a conscience?" she asked rhetorically, simultaneously waving her finger at the radio, which was reporting another news-breaking national scandal.

We often develop an impression of an individual, based on a slight misunderstanding. This mistake can color our

attitude towards that person forever after, simply because we put the wrong information in his file.

Even when we hear the words correctly, we can miss the meaning. They may have said it, but they did not necessarily intend what you heard.

49.

Time After Time

" **G** uess what. She missed it again."

"Oh, no. So that means you have to shlepp all the way there with her. That will take half an hour out of your morning."

"Well. What can I do?"

Get her to bed earlier. Keep her moving in the morning. Or just buy her an alarm clock. That's what I was thinking, but I held my tongue.

My sister-in-law's daughter had missed the bus again. That was the second time this week, and probably the 15th time this year. It did not really make sense to me, because Ellen, my sister-in-law, runs a tight ship. It's not the kind of home where no one can find anything, where sandwiches from last week are stuck to the inside of the book bags, or where you have to discreetly brush off the seat of a chair before sitting down. On the contrary, her house is immaculate and her children well-groomed. So I just could not understand why it was so hard for her to get that child on the bus.

My house is as busy as hers, probably even more so. Yet, my kids get up and dressed, finish eating, and are waiting outside for the bus well before it arrives each morning. Where was Ellen going wrong?

Of course, I never said a word and I really tried not to be judgmental. Two sides were battling it out in my mind. One side suggested that maybe her daughter needs a lot of sleep and is hard to awaken in the morning. Maybe she's not a morning person and moves slowly at that hour. But that other side of me kept persisting, *Why can't she just get her act together?*

Ellen and I spoke on the phone on a regular basis, and several more times throughout that year, she complained to me about having wasted half her morning getting her daughter to school. I sympathized with her but kept my thoughts to myself.

The school year ended. The summer passed. Somehow my daughter's internal time clock changed. Ever since infancy she had gotten up at the crack of dawn. For some reason, as winter approached, she began waking up at 7:15. Of course, I tried to get her up earlier, but she just could not open her eyes. And now, being one of the first bus stops, she had to be out there at 7:35. It does not take a genius to figure out that that means twenty minutes to get up, wash up, get dressed, make her bed, and grab some food. And sometimes the bus came early! As you may have figured out, I spent many a morning that year wasting half of it taking my daughter to school.

What happened to that simple advice I had offered Ellen? *Get her to bed earlier. Keep her moving in the morning. Or just buy her an alarm clock.*

❧

One of the obstacles of judging people favorably is our certainty that if we would be in that person's place, we would never behave that way.

— I do not care how much pressure you are under, there is no excuse for...

— Nothing would ever cause me to...

Ethics of the Fathers *2:5 tells us, "Don't judge your friend until you reach his place." We might one day find ourselves in "that place," and suddenly his behavior becomes quite comprehensible. It just takes "getting there" to get it.*

50.

The Ingrate

The story that I am about to relate was so shocking that I myself could hardly believe it, even though I was an eyewitness to the events.

When my cousin Naomi married Alex Brenner, he was a struggling young man without a penny to his name. Slowly, we saw him climb the ladder to financial success. Possessing sharp business acumen, he opened a wholesale liquidation business. As can be expected with all beginnings, he got off to a sluggish start, surmounting many difficulties with jealous competition. Step by arduous step, business began to boom.

Eventually, he opened another branch. And a few years later, another. By then my cousin's husband was considered a man of means. They call it nouveau riche. That's the title, and that describes their lifestyle. On the rare occasions I would visit — some family gathering or celebration — I took a peek into this world quite unfamiliar to me. From my vantage point, they had it all. In addition to the material plenty, Naomi and Alex had four darling children. Always big-hearted and exuding warmth, Naomi was extremely devoted to them. As you can imagine, her position thrust upon her a heavy social agenda and days and nights filled with philanthropic undertakings. She chaired benefits, planned teas, and coordinated Sisterhood luncheons. Naomi was willing to share her assets generously, whether it was her time, her resources, or her talents.

Apparently, she had been seeking the same good-heartedness in a mate, and Alex ended up filling that role perfectly.

He himself was no slouch in fulfilling his community responsibilities. I knew him more in the family circle, where his openhandedness was discussed with admiration. I clearly remember two family members fighting over an inheritance issue. Things were going from bad to worse. Neither side would budge. Both wives and some of the children joined in the fight and had stopped speaking. Alex stepped in behind the scenes and handed over the sum in question, just to restore the peace.

But if that story impresses you, just listen to this one.

When Naomi's brother, Nathan, was down and out, it was Alex who came to the rescue. Nathan had been jobless for months. Despite concerted efforts, he was floundering and just could not find himself a place. Slowly, he was falling into debt, not able to meet mortgage payments, or any other payments for that matter. Naomi was beside herself and appealed to Alex to help.

Sure enough, Alex came through in a big way. He gave Nathan one of his locations. He did not just offer him a management position. He actually signed it over to him. Maybe you could say that a man with that wealth can afford one branch less. But truthfully, how many people do you know would do that, even if they could afford to?

Nathan obviously wanted to prove himself to his brother-in-law and show him that he was a worthy and grateful recipient. He worked like a beaver and did well.

Years passed. Things were going well in the Brenner household, and the boys were growing up beautifully.

One morning before I left for work, the phone rang. It was a neighbor who was making the calls. Alex had suffered a massive heart attack. The funeral was scheduled for three in the afternoon.

My cousin tried her best to go on with her life. And let me tell you, that best was very good. It was as if she was doubling up on the warmth and love, taking over where her late husband could not. She was a terrific example for the children and bit by bit got them on their feet.

Naomi and I became closer and spoke often. We got together more frequently.

I don't know how it happened or exactly when, but life in that house was not the same, on many levels.

The maid was dismissed. The cleaning help was sent away. The second car was sold. I wondered, but said nothing. But when Naomi told me that she was thinking of looking for a job, I was more than a little surprised. What would she do? As far as I knew, she had no training.

Not long after, my wealthy cousin announced that she had taken a job as a saleslady in a local department store.

Over time, the truth came out. Nathan had taken over the finances, but literally. He was overseeing, managing, running the whole business in all of the locations. Naomi had been pushed out altogether. She was receiving no salary, no share in the earnings. Hadn't Alex made provisions for her and the children? Where was the insurance? What happened to his investments?

I asked family members. No one knew. They just knew that brother Nathan was a number one ingrate if there ever was one. Did I exaggerate when I said "shocking"? Imagine! Nathan had been drowning. Alex had pulled him out and set him on his feet. Look what Nathan owes his brother-in-law, and look how he paid back the debt.

Naomi, that princess, came through with flying colors. Another person dealt that deck would have had plenty to say. What was her reaction?

Bear witness to the lofty level to which a human being can rise. Naomi raised her children to respect and show honor to her brother at every occasion. They called, they visited, they remembered Uncle Nathan's birthday and anniversary. The uncle who had turned against them, abandoning them in their need and sorrow.

Naomi, a woman of valor, was repaid by Heaven for this exceptional generosity of spirit. Her children grew up and each one of them became an outstanding personality in his own right, men at the forefront of worthy community projects and charity organizations. In short, a *nachas* to their mother and to their People.

Now, dear readers, let us replay the last lines of this story, and you will learn the real meaning of "valor."

Let's replay it this way:

After Alex's death, the lawyers and accountants sat with the books for hours. They were appalled at what they were seeing. They checked and rechecked. As shocking as it was, the proof was there in black and white.

The hardest part was how to break it to Alex's wife. It was, however, unavoidable. Eventually, she would have to know. Alex had been heavily in debt. We are talking about big money. He kept it from everyone, hoping desperately to recoup his losses. He knew full well that if his true status got out, no one would extend credit. People would demand payment. Overnight, he would be finished.

When Naomi heard, she came to an instant decision. Alex's reputation should not be tarnished. He had passed away with a good name. She wanted it to remain that way.

She begged Nathan to take over. Any monies that were coming to her should be used to pay debts. Everything, every penny. She wanted nothing for herself. Her sole concern was for her husband's good name. She was healthy, capable. There was nothing wrong with her going out to earn a living with her own two hands.

And she brought up her boys to respect their uncle, the only one who knew the real story. The one who allowed himself to be cast as the villain, Uncle Nathan, was thankful to be able to repay his brother-in-law for all he had done for him.

❧

This is just one more story to illustrate our theme: Things are not always the way they seem.